# Developing the
# Junior Golfer

# Developing the Junior Golfer

## A GUIDE TO BETTER GOLF FOR STUDENTS AND PARENTS

*Brendan M. Ryan*

ISBN: 0692584021
ISBN 13: 9780692584026

# Bio for book

———✸———

BRENDAN RYAN IS THE OWNER of Golf Placement Services, a boutique business that provides specialized golf services in the areas of college placement and corporate recruiting. Brendan, a natural connector, has built an extensive international network of world renowned coaches, teachers and industry professionals. He uses this network on a daily basis to help students navigate the college search process and find schools that meet their individual academic, athletic, financial and social needs. In addition, he has also performed corporate recruiting projects for universities and golf academies.

This book contains ideas based on academic research and practical experience that Brendan has gained in his 15 years in the golf industry and in higher education. For many junior golfers and their parents, the ideas presented in this book will be new. Should you need help in understanding or applying them, please do not hesitate to contact Brendan via his website - www.golfplacementservices.com or via mobile at 407-233-6946.

*I would like to dedicate this book to my family; Anne Marie, Rory, Michael, Pat, Cathie, Bill, Patrick, Susan Kevin, Debbie, Frank and all my wonderful cousins. Each of you are tremendously important to me and I love you all.*

# Table of Contents

FOR THE PAST 15 YEARS I have lived my passion—competitive golf. I've been granted the unique opportunity to coach, teach, study and play among many great minds from the world of golf as well as from the general academic community. These experiences have enriched my understanding of the game and allowed me to provide extremely valuable advice to the students I mentor. Within these pages, the high-school golfer will find advice and guidance specific to their stage of life and to their dream of a college experience that includes competitive golf. For the adults who read this book, there are insights and observations that you are sure to need as you continue raising an educated and well-adjusted young golfer. I sincerely hope that what you read here will serve as a valuable reference in your journey.

# CHAPTER 1

# Developing a Plan

—⊷⊷⊷—

*"Our goals can only be reached through a vehicle of a plan, in which we must fervently believe, and upon which we must vigorously act. There is no other route to success."*

PABLO PICASSO?

## WHAT IS MEANT BY "DEVELOPING THE JUNIOR GOLFER"?

I COULD HAVE CHOSEN MANY other names for this book, but I settled on the title "Developing the Junior Golfer" because of the importance I attach to the word "development." This book is about a process. There are no quick fixes or simple tricks on the road to elite performance in golf. Instead, each idea must be carefully considered, with many development phases requiring long periods of extended effort. This may come as bad news, so I want to also share some good news: I have seen each of these ideas help students become better players and reach their goals. I believe you can do the same, if you are willing to take the appropriate steps!

The word "development" is a significant aspect of this book and of my belief system. Parents and athletes need to understand that development takes time and that golf is a game of peaks and valleys. In fact, during any year, it is likely that a student will play twice as many really bad weeks of golf as great weeks of golf. You must be prepared for this to happen - high and low points are expected along the journey.

Throughout the book, I will introduce you to researchers, thinkers, authors and friends. Each of these individuals has played a major role in my intellectual development. This book will expose you to many of their ideas and how you can use them to become a better junior golfer.

The first of these individuals is Dr. Daniel Kahneman, professor emeritus at Princeton University. Dr. Kahneman has spent his life looking at how people think and function and has developed a framework called System 1 and System 2. System 1 is what humans use most of the time to complete routine tasks; it is the autopilot: we use this to brush our teeth and tie our shoes. System 2 relates to our ability to think critically and analyze tasks. The problem is that many times when we should be using System 2, we are lazy and use System 1. The results are minor errors. To prove this point, I would like to use an example from his current bestselling book called, "Thinking, Fast and Slow": The problem is:

**A ball and a bat cost $1.10. The bat costs a dollar more than the ball. How much does the ball cost?**

Faced with this problem, many people quickly blurt out "10 cents," which is incorrect. The correct answer is 5 cents,

because in order for the bat to cost one dollar more than the ball, the price for the bat must be $1.05 (2x + 1 = 1.10 or x = .05).
But most peoples' minds quickly jump to a solution and the sum of $1.10 gets split into two entities, one being a dollar and the other being 10 cents—and each of those two numbers gets assigned to one of the two physical objects.

As this demonstrates, we humans are susceptible to heuristics, i.e., we tend to use shortcuts to solve problems quickly and efficiently. This is true in many things, including the game of golf. For the junior golfer and their parent, the biggest problem is a lack of understanding between perception of performance and actual performance. The common misconception is that the junior golfer is better than they are and simply had a bad tournament or poor luck or just needs to hit a few more balls to finally get that swing change under control. Junior golfers are not training to be outstanding tournament players. Instead they are training in ways that will likely lead to less than optimal tournament performance. This is a result of poor information that focuses mostly on building better golf swings, not better tournament golfers. The rest of this book is designed to fill the gap between these ideas and empower you with the information to create better practice plans, shoot lower scores and reach your long term potential.


## BASICS OF BALL CONTROL
Much of golf literature covers the technical "golf swing". This book is not about golf swing however I would like to acknowledge the importance of "ball control". Ball control is probably the most fundament skill in golf. Ball control is defined as the

ability to hit the ball where you are looking. It involves controlling the variables of shot shape, trajectory and spin.

Ball control is the result of good instruction and lots of practice. Players are advised to invest significant amounts of time and energy early in their career to develop the ability to control their ball. Early in their career is different for each player, depending on when they are introduced to the game. Whenever the time frame, you are well advised to spend 1-2 years on this aspect of the game. It is important to note that having ball control does not mean that you have a perfect looking golf swing. Instead it means that you are able to generate consistent results with a benchmark of 75% of the time.


## Danger on the Range

The driving range provides a place of great comfort for many golfers. It is where most of us took our first mighty rips at the small white ball. On the tee line we enjoy casual conversations, perfect lies and the distant range picker to fire shots at (with success signaled by that magical *ding!*). It's a place of optimism and small triumphs, well-designed to introduce new golfers to the game. However as I hope to show, the range is also a place of some danger.

For the young golfer who hits basket upon basket of striped balls, there is a chance of encountering significant development delays, even setbacks. Every junior golfer needs time on the range to build the skills of ball control. This task needs to continue until the player has reached a fairly high competency. However once the player has developed ball control, they should quickly turn their attention to the development of other skills such as the ones outlined throughout the rest of this book!

## SUMMARY

Much of what is available to the junior golfer and their parents speaks to golf swing and mechanics. Although this is an important part of development, it is not necessarily linked to performance. This book is designed to help educate players and parents about the various aspects of development which will hopefully help the player improve performance and reach their long term goals in golf.

# CHAPTER 2

# Selecting the Right Coach for Your Junior Golfer

———— ∞∞∞ ————

*"When you make a choice, you change the future."*

DEEPAK CHOPRA

## WHY DO YOU NEED A COACH?

DURING ASSESSMENTS OF JUNIOR GOLFERS, I often ask this question: If I gave you unlimited mulligans, what would you shoot? The usual answer is "54 or lower" (most players searching for scholarships have the ability to make a birdie on almost any hole). I then follow up by asking the junior what his or her best score is for 18 holes. Normally I hear 69-76. In that case, the gap between the potential and skill is from 15 to 22 strokes. The goal then becomes to help put together a plan to improve skills and scoring. The first step in this plan is helping to find someone to help guide you.

The psychologists David Dunning and Justin Kruger showed that people often overestimate their own competence. Their paper "Unskilled and Unaware of It" details their subjects failing to recognize a mismatch between their actual performance and their perception of their performance. This is exactly why the junior golfer (and their family) is wise to invest in working with a professional on their game. In this chapter we will detail the process of finding the right coach and teacher for the junior golfer.

## DIFFERENCE BETWEEN A COACH AND A TEACHER
We need to draw the distinction between a coach and a teacher. In the world of golf, there exists a huge disconnect between coaching and teaching and it is important to understand the difference.

**Coaching** is a holistic approach. Its functions include mental and emotional training for competition, strategic preparation for tournaments, golf course analysis, methods of proper practice, shot-making skill development and transference—even such offshoots as academic achievement and development of personal maturity.

**Teaching or Instruction** is much more tightly defined. It refers to technical development within the golf swing, the short game and putting, with an emphasis on club delivery and body motion.

When working with a teacher or coach, please keep in mind the following rules:

1. *A one hour lesson is an exchange of information between student and coach/teacher*

2. *A series of lessons is designed to help the student improve a particular skill*
3. *A long term commitment to an instructor or coach should result in both improved skill and lower scores*

Tournament golfers who have long term stable scores work towards mastery. They have a coach that teaches them skill and they work daily on refining this skill. Golfers with inconsistent results tend to work with a coach or teacher only when there are "problems" that need to be fixed. This is one of the major strategic differences that I see among different levels of tournament players.

## GAUGING THE SKILL LEVEL OF YOUR GOLFER

As you enter this process, it is important that you be educated about what your student-athlete might need in a long-term development coach. To go about gaining that education, you can do any of the following:

*Have your junior take a Trackman Combine:* This is a test in which you hit 6 shots to 9 targets ranging from 60 to 180 yards as well as 6 drives. The test consists of 60 shots; players hit six shots to 9 different targets at 60, 70, 80, 90, 100, 120, 140, 160, 180 yards plus six drives. Shots are scored on a scale of 0-100. This is all done under the scrutiny of the Trackman 3d ball flight analysis which automatically measures deviation from the target and allocates the score. The scores are averaged and at the conclusion you receive a net score of 0 to100.

Here are some feedback ranges on Trackman scoring -

- 0-50    Very low.  Needs technical skill development and increased ball control
- 50-60:  Below average. Certain areas may need significant work
- 60-70:  Average
- 70-75:  Junior tournament golfer
- 75+:    College golfer on scholarship

The cost of this experience is about $70 for the 35-minute test.

*Enroll your junior in stats analysis using Shot by Shot:* I would recommend using the program Shot by Shot for at least a two or three months. It allows the golfer to track key stats from GIR to Strokes Gained to Up-and-Down percentage. By collecting this information you will have a good sense of the student-athlete's strengths and weaknesses, which will be important in understanding what you might need in a coach. Cost is $79 per year.

*Interview potential instructors and coaches:*  Now that you know more about your student-athlete, it is time to start the process of trying to connect with the right person. Before you call, I recommend that you look at the results of the information carefully and consider the areas that need improvement. Based on these areas, come up with questions that would be appropriate. For example, if your student-athlete has performed poorly on the Trackman Combine test and has poor greens-in-regulation stats, then you probably want someone with technical ability to help improve ball control and club delivery. On the other hand, if your student-athlete has good stats and Combine results, but struggles with on-course scoring, then you want someone who can help with practice plans and understand concepts like transference.

## AN INTRO TO 3 COMMON TYPES OF TEACHERS

### 1. THE NUMBERS GUY

We live in a golf renaissance; today we have more information and technology then every before in the history of golf. Included in this technology are systems like Trackman and Golf 3d software. There are also those coaches who have become experts in interpreting the numbers these machines generate; they give feedback based on the data provided. The strength of these teachers in junior development is to help students develop ball control.

### 2. THE METHOD TEACHER

This label, created by Jim Mclean, is one of the harshest labels that a golf pro can receive. Method teachers have a model swing and work towards giving everyone the same elements in their swing. Results from these teachers can vary significantly; some pupils might have significant success, however some will get significantly worst because the elements might not work with other aspects of their swing.

Avoid these types of teachers.

3. The System Teacher

System teaching is another term that can be credited to Jim McLean. In this model, teachers work within a "window" of acceptable patterns. For example, students might be able to have some aspects of their swing that are not ideal; however they do not need to change all aspects of their swing to improve. They can improve certain aspects while maintaining other aspects.

I would most encourage junior golfers and their families to seek a system teacher because they will help the student work to improve, without having to "overhaul" or "re-do" their swing (any time you hear this, run!). Instead they will provide specific feedback on patterns that impact performance. They will then outline changes in these areas.

## What Skills do Outstanding Teachers/Coaches Possess?

1. They teach skills using a plan. That plan involves diagnosis, prescription and execution. Skill is not only technical, but also involves emotional, physical and tactical development.
2. They understand motivation
3. They believe in education
4. They communicate with energy, imagination and precision
5. They watch their student-athletes compete
6. They emphasize that the solution to the student's issues lie with the student

## What should an outstanding teacher/coach expect of their student-athlete?

1. Goals: A vision of what the student-athlete wants to accomplish
2. Passion
3. Grit
4. Accountability
5. Desire to learn

## Responsibilities of coach/teacher to the student-athlete

1. To understand the needs of the student-athlete and possess the skills necessary to help them reach their goals
2. To effectively communicate with the student-athlete and all other stakeholders, describing the process and all expectations. This includes a specific plan of improvement with timelines and goals that are measurable, realistic and attainable.
3. To effectively communicate the role of development within the model of competition and the player's long-term goals.
4. To observe the student-athlete in environments beyond the driving range, so as to gain better insight into the student-athlete, their motivation and any gaps in their skills. Note: Player skills can be technical, emotional, psychological and tactical.

5. To support in creating an environment where the student-athlete can achieve their desired outcome. This environment should be competitive, fun, challenging and supportive.
6. To effectively communicate with other stakeholders so that each plays the appropriate role in the student-athlete's life and development.

RESPONSIBILITIES OF THE STUDENT IN THE COACH-STUDENT RELATIONSHIP

1. Must effectively communicate to the coach their goals for the relationship
2. Must have ownership of the process including investing proper time in implementation of the plan and effectively communicating their experience of "living" the plan.
3. Must be willing to explore ideas outside of their comfort zone
4. Must execute the long-range plan in a manner that is conducive to success

QUESTIONS TO ASK WHEN INTERVIEWING A COACH

1. What experience do you have?
2. Where does your knowledge come from? How did you acquire it?
3. What are your values?

4. How often do you watch your student's on-course and/ or give playing lessons?
5. Is there a program? How does it work?
6. What do you expect of the student-athlete?
7. What should we expect of you?
8. What have you done to educate yourself this year? How many days was that program?
9. Do you have a model? What is it? How would my student-athlete fit that model?
10. Do you have written plans for your student-athletes? Can we see an example?
11. Have you worked with a similar level player in the past? What was the result? Why do you think it worked that way?

## STOCK SHOT

A stock shot is also known as a "go-to" shot. It is different for everyone and based on their personal preference. For example, I have always hit a draw. I feel most comfortable in competition using that shot.

I am continually surprised watching junior golf that so few students understand this concept. I think a major part of being a great player is having a shot that, when all else is going wrong, you can count on. If you want to compete and win, be sure you've got a go-to shot in your arsenal.

## WATCHING GOLF

A key part of development occurs when a coach watches their student-athlete play golf. I can't tell you how many teachers never see their students perform on the course in competition. Observing first-hand how the student-athlete transfers technical skills from the range to competition is extremely important (and something we will speak a lot about in this book!). Without it, you are hard-pressed to prescribe a plan moving forward or make adjustments to previously crafted plans.

## THE TRICKY BUSINESS OF LIKABILITY

Likeability can be a tricky part of the coach-student relationship. Connecting well on a personal basis and being able to develop the abilities of the student-athlete is not the same thing. As the player develops, it is important that they have a coach/instructor who has the skills necessary to help build a long term development plan. This plan should include exactly what the player needs to do to reach their goals.

Jim McLean, a world expert on golf instruction, says that being a successful teacher is easily gauged; the best teachers make people better! Regardless of your personal feelings, the coach must help the player build effective results. If they do not, then it is important to have serious communication about the process, which in some cases might need to involve switching coaches.

## WHY GOOD PLAYERS CAN STRUGGLE TO BECOME EFFECTIVE COACHES

It is commonly felt that the best players have an edge when it comes to successful teaching and coaching. The idea is that they must know what it takes to be a successful tournament golfer because they, themselves, achieved that status. But having the information on how to play well and communicating that knowledge so that people understand it easily from their own perspective, and can apply it to their practice wherever they are on the learning curve, is crucial.

You may be sitting in your living room watching a lesson on the Golf Channel and someone may be telling you how to hit a cut shot. What they do may work for them, but if they can't communicate what it is they do to produce that shot so that everyone can digest it and use it in their training then they lack a core teaching-coaching skill. This analysis is supported by research conducted by Eric Mazur of Harvard who has found that as you become an expert in something, your models become more complex and the component steps that compose them fade into memory, making them difficult to describe.

## THE TWO-DAY CERTIFICATION

It is important to understand that many of the popular certifications that golf pros advertise are earned in training seminars that last only a few days. The seminars typically involve several hours of lecture and maybe some practical learning. However in most cases they have minimal testing with a huge majority (95%) earning certification. When considering a coach, I would encourage you to ignore the certifications all together.

GIVE A MAN A FISH AND YOU FEED HIM FOR A DAY. TEACH
A MAN TO FISH AND YOU FEED HIM FOR A LIFETIME.
It is extremely important that the athlete does not become
reliant on the coach for information, or, even worse, reliant on
the coach in order to perform. As the player progresses, it is
important that the coach help the player understand their patterns and tendencies. It is also important for the player to be
engaged in the solution and understand how different ideas
relate in the golf swing. This creates a healthy relationship.

In my years of working in junior golf, I have seen a lot of un-
healthy relationships where the player is very dependent on the
coach for information. This is developed by hours spent together,
where the coach / teacher provides feedback on every shot, often in intricate detail. The player becomes focused on this information more than on the result of the shot, which sets up a
pattern that's riddled with problems.

It is healthy when learning a new skill for the instructor to
provide feedback. However it is also important that the student understand the concept and be able to understand the
change, why the change happened, the next steps and the
time between introduction of the idea and implementation.

It is also important for the coach or teacher to explain the
basics of ball flight to the student. They should also make sure
the student understands their own tendencies and what pattern to look for when things are going wrong, as well as what
to do when it happens. It is important to note that this particular aspect of development can be extremely time-consuming.

However, it is extremely important in development—students must have ownership of their ball control if they are going to spend extend time playing tournament golf as a college player or a tour player.

## SUMMARY

For parents and juniors, an important step is selecting a coach/teacher to help guide you in the process. This chapter will help you understand what you might need in a coach, as well as the proper way to seek and find the right person to fit your needs.

CHAPTER 3

# Building Skills to Improve

———— ᴔᴔᴔ ————

*"We make our discoveries through our mistakes:*
*we watch one another's success: and where there is*
*freedom to experiment there is hope to improve."*

*- Arthur Quiller-Couch*

## Get familiar with Dr. Rick Jensen's "4 Steps to Mastery"

Dr. Rick Jensen is a performance consultant and sports psychologist, whose golf clients alone have won nearly 200 pro tour events. Within his large body of work is a formula that I particularly like called "4 Steps to Mastery". Here's a brief summary of it, along with my own thoughts on application. Each example assumes that the instructor is trying to teach the student how to hit a "draw" shot.

Understanding cause and effect is the first in this quartet of steps. It generally calls for the coach or teacher to explain a particular skill to the student. In the case of a student whose goal is to draw the ball on command, the teacher would break that skill down into its constituent parts. He or she would state that club face angle is about 80 percent responsible for the initial direction of the shot. Next, the coach would explain that the path-to-face-angle relationship, combined with centeredness of contact, determines the flight. The coach would be sure to point out that a well-executed draw shot does not cross the central aiming line established at setup.

In my experience, most golfers make an error in not understanding the cause and effect of the swing. This becomes a problem during development when the player goes to play several weeks of tournament golf. During this time the player starts to struggle with an aspect of their game and this causes several bad scores in a row because the player is not able to self-correct.

Supervised Practice, the second of the four steps, is what the name suggests—the teacher is watching as the student executes a drill. As the student performs the skill, the teacher studies the feedback provided by ball flight, impact sound, shape of divot and so forth. If a certain shot had too much draw, the teacher might ask: What did you notice? The student might reply that the shot curved more than desired. The coach would then ask "Why?" It would be up to the student to understand if the cause was more a face-to-path issue or a problem with centeredness of contact. This would continue until the student demonstrated to the teacher a sound understanding of the principals.

In some cases, the student might not demonstrate understanding. If so, the teacher must return to step 1 and make sure the student fully understands cause and effect. For many complex skills, this could take several attempts, but that's to be expected at times and the repetition is time well invested.

Transference training is Jensen's third step of four. This takes place on the golf course with the student attempting to include the new skill in his repertoire. Again using the example of draws, it may mean that the student plays all 18 holes hitting draws to every pin. As a golfer's overall skill level increases, the challenge of this third-step assignment needs to become more intense. In other words, the better the player, the harder the on-course exercise.

Play is the fourth and final step. Having completed his transference training, the student has nothing left to do except apply the new skill to a live round of golf. To Jensen, mastery implies self-diagnostic ability and self-correction, real-time. If the student tries to hit a draw and produces something closer to a pull-hook, he should have a very sound idea of the technical error that made this happen. He should be able to keep this understanding in mind so that he can devote part of his next training session to further building and honing the skill.

If you are a junior golfer or parent, you might notice that this process is significantly different from what you have experienced in your lessons; most often golf professionals give information ("tips") and the lesson is over. Long term, this method will lead to performance issues because the player has not really learned the skill!

## FAILURES AND MATURITY

Benjamin Franklin once wrote that there are two certainties in human life: death and taxes. I would add a third certainty: failure. For golfers, failure is a major part of development because of the amount of skills and the time necessary to gain experience. For example, in the skill of chipping there are countless trajectories produced by different ball positions for numerous lies on a number of different types of grass. Such a skill will take thousands of hours to master, so along the way don't worry about some failures; they are a completely normal part of development and should not be seen in any other way!

## How Long Should it take to get Better?

The brain functions in ways we don't always recognize. Think of a time when you worked for hours trying to solve a problem, eventually becoming frustrated or exhausted and walking away. You may have decided to quit for the day or just take a long break and do something enjoyable. Time passes and, seemingly out of nowhere, the solution to the problem occurs to you. What you have just experienced is the incubation effect.

The incubation effect is well-known and was included in an early four-stage theory of creativity, put forward in 1926 by Graham Wallas, an English psychologist who co-founded the London School of Economics. Wallas laid out his four stages thusly:

1. Preparation
2. Incubation
3. Illumination or insight
4. Verification

The problem with this theory is that the incubation phase is extremely mysterious. First you prepare and then you incubate which involves making no conscious effort to solve the problem, and then along comes the insight. Whether it sounds too good to be true or not, the psychological research backs up the common experience that incubation (or taking a break) does work. About 50 different studies have been carried out on the incubation effect and three-quarters of them prove its significance

For golfers this has an enormous impact. It tells us that after deliberate practice, we must allow our experience and our new information to incubate. We must understand that this is an organic, individual process and we must allow time. As might be expected, more incubation time becomes necessary as the material and experiences we've undergone become more complex.

For the parents of junior golfers, it is important to understand that developing a new skill requires some incubation. Unfortunately, at present, it is impossible to say how much time. What I can say from experience is that frustration or impatience does not help the process; it is important for the parent to understand that the nature of golf is difficult and will be riddled with many good and bad days. This is not cause for panic, but rather just the nature of the game.

## Instant Gratification vs Delayed Gratification

During the 1960s and early 70s, a researcher at Stanford University named Walter Mischel conducted an interesting test at a local nursery school. Mischel offered children a choice between receiving one treat that they could enjoy immediately or receiving two treats if they were willing to wait. The treats offered were cookies, marshmallows and pretzels. They were kept visible to the children, and those who initially chose the delayed double reward were instructed that if they no longer wished to wait they merely had to ring a bell to call the experimenter back. They also knew that there would be no second treat if they did this. A record was made of the results and follow-up research was conducted. The result? The longer a child delayed gratification, Mischel found—that is, the longer he or she was able to wait—the better they would fare later in life at numerous measures of what is called executive function. Students who displayed a preference towards delaying gratification were found to have better SAT scores, higher educational attainment, lower body mass index and other significant life measures.

Instant gratification is rampant in today's society. There is a trend toward not allowing the periods of percolation and digestion that help individuals learn and improve on a long-term basis. It is my observation that golf, in particular, has a long digestion time because there are a lot of variables. Student-athletes and their parents need to understand that getting scores down to the desired level might be a three-month process and that during this time it may become easy to revert back to other ways of achieving the desired results that can throw the player off track.

Too many people are misguided by the belief that in golf there is a secret to playing well. We all know the folklore of the

"Hogan Secret." But people are delusional about the ability to skip steps in order to get better. Any time someone tries to circumvent a step to achieve short-term success it leads to a breakdown in their game long-term. They may have some short-term success, but it usually comes apart over time because they haven't followed the proper steps and put in the practice on the right things to achieve long term goals.

I wish instructors would place more emphasis on skill development in young golfers and less on score. Many youngsters worry that, if their scores don't align with those of the players at a college they wish to attend, then they won't have the opportunity to play there, and that isn't productive or healthy. This emphasis on score feeds the trend toward instant gratification.

## WHY THE HIGH-SCHOOL GOLFER DOESN'T NEED A SPORTS PSYCHOLOGIST

When parents talk about their student-athlete needing a sports psychologist, I'm always taken aback. First and foremost, such a comment is destructive because it sends a clear signal to the player that a major part of their support system doubts their ability. In my opinion, this alone can be a major shock to the student-athlete and can significantly impact performance.

In my opinion, student-athletes rarely need help with their psychology. Instead most need help with their sports development plan because they suffer from fluency-over-transference; too much block practice makes transfer of range skills to the golf course very difficult. Remember that golf is a game of multiple, unique and concurrent shots. Range practice only helps with the "multiple" part.

What is most important is the desire to compete, to improve on a daily basis, using quantitative performance statistics, feedback from head-to-head competition and feedback from those experiences that leads to appropriate continued training. That is why you must embrace competition, because it is the best means to test yourself and test your skills.

An athlete must be given the opportunity to face real competition. For many, this is best done at the local country club with players of similar ability. This provides them opportunities to compete and most importantly endure loss, overcome intimidation and become psychologically familiar with competition.

## GOLF OCD

Obsessive-compulsive disorder is a mental condition marked by obsessive thoughts that lead to repetitive behaviors. We generally associate OCD with constant hand washing and paralyzing indecision about which objects to keep or discard. I believe that many golfers, particularly junior golfers, suffer from a version of OCD that is characterized by an obsession with swing patterns and small details of technique. The colloquial terminology for this is "golf swing over golf score".

Junior golfers must be very careful in their development to understand the role of ball control vs. scoring. Again, ball control is an important part of your long term development and should be taken seriously. However becoming obsessed with your golf swing is not healthy because eventually you will need to travel to a course and shoot scores!

## SUMMARY

A key theme of this book is the development of skills in order to shoot great tournament rounds and earn a college golf scholarship. The best framework to develop skill is the one presented in this book by Dr. Jensen. I would encourage student athletes and parents to use Dr. Jensen's work as a guideline. It is equally important that parents and juniors understand that the development cycle of junior golf is arduous; players take years, not months, to build proficiency in different areas.

# CHAPTER 4

# The Importance of Practice

———— ∞∞ ————

*"We are what we repeatedly do. Excellence,*
*then, is not an act, but a habit."*

*- ARISTOTLE*

## 10,000 HOURS / 20-YEAR LIFESPAN

ANDERS ERICSSON IS A PROFESSOR of psychology at Florida State University in Tallahassee.  Dr. Ericsson has published a paper analyzing the development of elite performers in music. What he noticed is that the best performers had the most hours of practice. He also noticed that they "acquire their superior performance and skills through extended, deliberate practice." Deliberate practice is defined as high concentration practice beyond one's comfort zone. In particular the highest performers had reached between 7,000 to 12,000 hours of practice by the age of 20 (this concept was also popularized by Malcolm Gladwell in his book, *Outliers*).  Ericsson stresses that these practice hours must be directed at the edge of the player's ability, making the environment uncomfortable and increasing the gains. For golfers this means that they must make practice tough and involve a consequence. For example, if you are working on putting, you should not stand in one spot hitting the small putt, raking balls into place. Instead you should move around the hole, making putts with a specific goal. When you reach the goal, you should stop and next time make the drill harder; possibly repeat with putts that break. If you do not reach your goal, there should be a consequence like push-ups or running or another skill related to your overall improvement.

When you understand the concept of practice, you know that no habits or skills can be developed without many repetitions of the behavior that improve that habit or skill. In addition and most critically, the desired movement or behavior must be positively reinforced during the building of habits. However, repetition alone is not sufficient. It is the identification of gaps in skill, followed by proper development of mastery that separate average and elite golfers.

To reiterate, **it is not repetitions alone that make the difference**. I have known avid golfers who practiced for over 30 years, and they are no better today than they were 30 years ago. All that practice did not lead to expert status. It only resulted in improving the already demonstrated skill. It is feedback and the reinforcement for improvement associated with the repetitions that make the difference.

What about genetic factors – i.e., those factors which we understand as being opposite to so-called acquired traits? Do they play a significant role in the development of elite performers?  The answer seems to be yes, in sports like running, where Vo2 output is strongly correlated to success at the elite level. The genetic factor is far less relevant in sports like golf. At the top levels of golf there are major gaps in physical talent. On one end is a Dustin Johnson, who can dunk a basketball and easily perform one-legged squats; on the other, is Eric Compton who competes in the PGA after **two** full heart transplants. (http://www.erikcompton.com/). At this point in golf, several players have become world-class without being extremely physically gifted. Instead these players invested long hours of deliberate practice into the sport and eventually reached the top. I think this makes the sport unique; people who otherwise are not physically gifted have the chance to excel.

## TYPES OF PRACTICE: BLOCK AND RANDOM

The vernacular of golf coaching and development includes the terms "random" and "block" practice. In block practice, individuals rehearse the same skill over and over until some improvement is seen. Random practice involves practicing multiple and unique skills in a random sequence. This type of practice would more closely mirror the actual game of golf.  It is important to understand the pros and cons of each type of practice.

# BLOCK PRACTICE
## *Pros:*

- Very important in early development
- Helps build confidence

## *Cons:*

- Can be boring
- Can lead to over-confidence
- After certain amount of block practice, player suffers from a diminishing return
- Less competitive player embraces this type of practice

# RANDOM PRACTICE
## *Pros:*

- Helps builds transference – ability to use acquired skill when needed on course
- Player hits unique shots – practice more interesting and fun
- More competitive player will embrace this type of practice

## *Cons:*

- Only useful if player has already done the block practice to acquire sufficient skills

## THOUGHTS ON BLOCK AND RANDOM PRACTICE

As described above, block practice in golf is the repeated striking of a certain shot with a certain club. It is favored by people with less experience as a path toward the mastery of skill. Our example is the newer golfer who stands on the range for an hour hitting 7-irons at the 150 yard marker.

In terms of development, this is a useful way to establish a pattern, using repetition. It is indeed necessary, especially early in the development of ball control. However, block practice has shortcomings because playing golf involves not only multiple shots of the same type, but also unique shots.

For most junior golfers, they can do it, however they often struggle producing under the stress of tournament golf. When this happens, I immediately question the type of preparation of the athlete and especially if they have spent too much time doing block practice. Random practice is the process of attempting shots of all different types, one after another. It better mirrors real golf by encouraging the player to hit multiple, unique and concurrent shots (just like a round).

## WHY YOUR "RANGE GAME" DOESN'T TRANSLATE TO THE COURSE

Golfers have been trained to believe that practice means hitting a bucket of balls on the range. I am here to say that this idea is incomplete. Hitting multiple shots at a target, for example 7-irons at the 150-yard post, builds fluency. The problem is that under pressure conditions of tournament golf, golfers don't have the skills necessary to perform. Why? Because fluency, hitting good shots on the range, does not mean that someone can perform on the course under stress. The art of taking the range to the golf course is called transference. Transference is putting skills into practice. A key fact for students and parents to understand is that beating 4-irons at a flag on a range and dialing that shot in, doesn't mean that skill will work next time you play golf. **Instead, more likely, striking balls well on the range gives you the misconception that you have mastered the skill.** It is this illusion of competency that many golfers need to fight in order to improve and be able to transfer their skills to tournament play.

## The World Beyond the Range

The range is an important place and should be used as a tool, especially in the development of ball control. However the junior golfer must be aware of transferring their skills from the range to the golf course. In order to help with this process, I would like to introduce you a couple examples of how I used the golf course with former players in order to help them perform better in tournaments.

CASE STUDY A – "Player A" with lots of length who is struggling with their par-5 scoring.

After reviewing stats during a meeting, Player A and I discovered a gap in their par-5 scoring. This player was very talented, with a lot of length; however the stats showed she was not using her length to generate birdies on the par 5's. The first thing we did was figure out her average distance to the hole on her second shot. This was between 235-260 yards. We then allowed her to play holes only from these distances. This allowed her to develop several skills. The first skill was hitting these shots on the greens. The second skill was deciding when to attempt to hit on the green and when to lay-up. If the shot was a lay-up, then she had to decide how far to leave herself and what angle (this eventually became its own game!).

<u>CASE STUDY B</u> – "Player B" with a poor record of making birdies inside 100 yards.

After reviewing stats during a meeting, Player B and I discovered a gap in her wedge game. She was only getting up and down from inside 100 yards, 8 percent of the time. After the meeting, I asked her to play nine holes from between 50 and 100 yards and play each hole as a par-3 with the goal of shooting 3-under on those holes.

I did similar things with entire teams throughout my time as a coach. In an analysis of one of my teams during a particular semester, I noted that we had problems with 3-putts and hitting greens. I carefully considered these elements and called a meeting of the players. I announced that, in our qualifying sessions, we would play Drawback on the greens during our first round and during our second round we would play the GIR game. In the GIR game, each player hit from the fairway until they landed a ball on the green. Each attempt counted as a stroke towards their score. On a par-4 where they hit the fairway, they would play their approach and head to the green, if their attempt was successful. Then if they two-putted they would score a 4 for the hole. If their approach shot missed, and then a second attempt missed, but their third approach shot was successful, a two-putt would result in a 6 for that hole.

This approach allowed me to understand whether a team member suffered from an issue of fluency (the ability to do it) or from an issue of transference (the ability to do it right now). At the end of a weekend of qualifying, I had a lot more data about the team and was able to formulate two different practice plans for the players, based on their weaknesses.

## GAMES TO HELP TRANSFER SKILLS TO THE GOLF COURSE

**WORST BALL:** Hit two balls on every shot and play the worst of the two until you complete the hole. A score of two over par for a round is an exceptionally good performance. This game is great for players who are at the peak of their game and looking for a challenge.

**G-I-R:** Hit a drive and from wherever you land, try and hit the green. If you don't hit the green, hit another shot until you do hit the putting surface, with each shot contributing to a score on the hole. This game is great for players looking to hit more greens. As we know from the work of Peter Sanders, founder of Shot by Shot, proximity to the hole and greens in regulation are closely correlated to score.

**DRAWBACK:** On the green, if you miss your first putt, draw the ball a putter's length back from the hole. This is a great drill because succeeding at this game will require strong lag putting, as well as the need to make lots of shorter putts. Often for tournament players this is an aspect of the game that goes underappreciated.

**THREE CLUBS AND A PUTTER:** Choose three clubs and a putter and play a hole. This will teach you to hit different shot trajectories, and shape shots from varying distances. It will improve your control of the clubface and your body motion, and help you understand how your body works in relation to the power you generate. This game is an excellent opportunity for someone who needs to learn to hit different shots. Many athletes who play at a country club get into the habit of playing the same tees, which, if they are skilled, leaves them a lot of similar shots. This game and others like it will give you an opportunity to hit a variety of different shots.

**KICK, THROW AND RE-TEE:** During a round against an opponent, you can kick or throw your opponent's ball or have him re-tee upon your choosing. Usually, I would say it works best if you allow one of each interruption per round. It's a game that sometimes get vicious, but it is a fantastic game that teaches you to embrace bad luck and deal with it in a specific way in order to make the best score you can. It also teaches you to control your emotions. If a coach sees his student-athlete stripe one down the fairway 330 yards, he is definitely going to ask him to re-tee. It poses a highly relevant question: You can do it, sure—but can you do it again?

This is a great game to help the student build emotional control and competitiveness. It can also be played in a variety of ways between players of different skill levels to make matches more competitive.

**ONE CLUB AND A PUTTER:** This is an especially good game on shorter holes; let's say a 360-yard par-4. If I hit my 5-iron 185 yards, then I have to hit two very good shots to reach the green in regulation, which teaches consistency. Say a student-athlete chooses a 4-iron and a putter on a hole that measures from 330 to 400 yards in length.  If he hits a bad shot off the tee, he will be faced with a difficult shot with the same club, perhaps over a bunker to a pin just behind it. This is another great game for ball control and puts pressure on the player to hit quality golf shots. It also tests the player's ability to make and execute plans.

**WORST-BALL CHIPPING:**  Hit two chips near the green and play the worst one. This puts pressure on the student-athlete to hit consistently good shots, knowing that any poor shot will be penalized severely. This is a great game for players who are working on transference in chipping.

**AIM FOR BUNKERS:** From the fairway hit the ball into the bunker on every hole and see how that affects your score. This is a great game for players working on transference in bunker play, as well as iron play.

**PAR-THREE GAME:** Play every hole as a par-three. You do this at whatever distance works for you, whether it is from 30 to 70 yards or 140 to 170 yards. We often play between 100 and 190 yards and go back down. Do this for 18 holes. It is good practice because it simulates shots that you will face in completion. This is a great game for players working on transference in their iron game. Please note that you can play this at any yardage. For example I was, for many years, a terrible player from 175-200 yards, so I spent a lot of time playing games from that yardage.

**PAR-FIVE GAME:** Play every hole as a par-5, finding your average distance from the green on a par-5 with your approach shot and measuring that distance to the flag. It's interesting to do this on par-4s because the holes were not designed as par-5s and it brings in all sorts of variables, such as bunkering. This teaches you when you can go for the green in two or when you should lay up. It also helps with transference on decision-making, as well as on long shots into the green.

**LAY-UP:** Play every hole as a par-4 and lay up to a certain yardage. This teaches you to practice control of your ball off the tee, which gives you the ability to practice distance control and understand how far the ball will carry and roll out. For better players, do this without a tee, because it teaches the need to be extraordinarily accurate in order to control the shot and distance. This helps with transference on distance control off the tee.

**BIRDIE EVERY HOLE:** Simply play a hole until you birdie it. This is best done in a golf cart and when the course is not busy. This helps with transference of hitting enough good shots to make birdies and builds grit.

NOTE: Obviously, some of these games should be played only when the opportunity presents itself. If you do this on a Saturday morning you are going to get kicked off the golf course. These games are best done at 4 o'clock on a Tuesday afternoon. Some can be done within the confines of a normal round if the course is not too busy.


## PLAYING THE COURSE ON THE RANGE

During my time as a coach, I have often suggested that my players use part of their range session during a warm up to play the first couple of holes of the course. This means taking the score card, picking specific targets and shots and then on the range hitting the different shots in sequence, as if they were playing those first few holes.   By doing this, the player has the opportunity to get comfortable with the shots they will have to make at the beginning of their round.

# 275/2/3

Based on 15 years of work with college players and elite juniors, I have concluded that elite college golf requires a commitment of at least 275 days per year. Based on this, I advocate that juniors work towards a program of 275/3/2; that means that on 275 days each year, they spend a total of three hours per day devoted to two activities: golf and fitness.

## RCGA DEVELOPMENT PLAN

One of the best documents produced on junior golf is the Royal Canadian Golf Association Long Term Development Plan. It is available free online (http://www.rcga.org/_uploads/documents/Player%20Development/LTPD/Golf_In_Canada_low.pdf) and I would recommend every parent use it as a resource to help their student athlete understand the type and amount of practice they should be engaged in.

One key point in the document that I would like to point out is an emphasis on what the RCGA terms "contacts". Every time the club face strikes the ball, (including putter face), that's a contact, be it in practice or on-course play. This takes in every practice putt of every length, every chip, pitch, middle iron, hybrid, fairway wood or driver strike. So, here's a question for every college bound student-athlete, age 16 or older, reading this book: How many contacts do you make per week? How many do you think you should make?

Write down your number here:

_____

Now consider that according to this document, you should make between 1,650 and 2,650 a week for elite junior golfers. That comes to 235 per day, on the low end. Is this how much you are doing?

## SUMMARY

Practice is the most important part of building skill. In this chapter, I have provided information about not only the amount of practice, but also the type of practice you should engage in to lower scores. I hope this will allow you to be more efficient with your time and lead to better scores.

## CHAPTER 5

# The Importance of Competition

*"It is not the critic who counts; not the man who points out how the strong man stumbles, or where the doer of deeds could have done them better. The credit belongs to the man who is actually in the arena, whose face is marred by dust and sweat and blood; who strives valiantly"*

*- THEODORE ROOSEVELT*

## COMPETITION AND GOLF

ONE OF THE CRUCIAL ASPECTS in the development of a young golfer is that he or she possesses a love of competition. The most successful players that I deal with will always go to the first tee and want to know what they are playing for! In terms of development, if you don't have that desire to truly test yourself in competition, or if, conversely, you fear competition, you are in trouble.

Competition and its role in performance were first studied by Norman Triplett of Indiana University. In 1897, Dr. Triplett examined the Racing Board of the League of American Wheelmen, trying to examine race times of cyclists against the clock and cyclists against other cyclists. He concluded that the competition of racing against another cyclist took five seconds per mile less than racing against a clock. These are interesting findings because sport has a unique place in society; it's the only non-military setting in which people unabashedly attempt to beat one another. Children as young as three know how to compete, says Ernst Fehr, an Austrian researcher.

## Nervous vs. Excited

What we think of as emotions are impulses and energies governed by the limbic system of the brain and the autonomic nervous system. Skilled, competitive young golfers, whether playing a tournament or practicing, should feel some kind of emotional energy or charge. Our everyday language doesn't have particularly apt names for the various sensations our central nervous systems produce. As a result, the vague adjective "nervous" tends to get overused. That's a linguistic trap, one I urge players and parents to avoid. When the young player feels a charge of energy running through him or her, they can identify it as "nerves" or they can choose to view it as "excitement." If you are locked into the proper competitive mindset, you should feel that energy *as excitement!*

## 9 HOLES VS 18 HOLES

It's important for a junior's development to play 18-hole rounds. Golf is a game of multiple, sequential and unique shots and is often played in tournaments of 36 holes in junior golf and 54 holes in college golf. It is important that players at all levels engage in the opportunity to play lots of holes without interruption in order to build skills like physical endurance, mental toughness and understand nutrition/hydration needs.

## NATIONAL JUNIOR SCORE GOLF RANKINGS

To get a ranking a player must play 4 events within 365 days. For these rounds remember that 75% of your ranking comes from your score compared to the course rating and how you finish in the tournament. Players need to be prepared to play tournaments because their score is going to count for their ranking and ranking is going to help coaches narrow the list of people that they are considering for scholarships.

## AMERICAN JUNIOR GOLF ASSOCIATION

Started in 1978, the American Junior Golf Association gives junior golfers the opportunity to experience competitive tournament golf, as the AJGA conducted approximately 116 tournaments for young players, ages 12-19, across the continental United States. Most junior golfers join the AJGA to not only learn how to play tournament golf, but many also hope to be seen by college golf coaches and secure a golf scholarship.

Joining the AJGA can be done online at www.ajga.org. Juniors must be at least 12 years of age to participate in an AJGA event. An amateur golfer who is 18 years old on January 1 is eligible for the entire calendar year, provided they graduate high school that year. Once a player starts college they are no longer considered a junior golfer regardless of age.

Prior to applying to your first tournament or qualifier, you will need to submit acceptable proof-of-age documentation to the AJGA. A copy of either a birth certificate, passport or driver's license is acceptable documentation. This document can be mailed or emailed to the AJGA.

# How to Play in the AJGA

## Join as a playing member
2017 Schedule comes out around the week of Sept 19 (early sign-up begins in October; you should sign up by Thanksgiving to start entering early events, as some deadlines are December and January.)

All players receive one Performance Star when they join or renew their membership with the AJGA to give them an initial status. High school sophomores and seniors receive one additional membership Performance Star (two total). High school juniors receive two additional membership Performance Stars (three total). A player will retain any Performance Stars received for membership for the entire season.

*Please note: these **Performance Stars** gained from signing up are not cumulative from year-to-yea, however stars that are earned in junior golf do carry over to the following year.*

Members can play a <u>maximum of five Open and/or Junior All-Star Series tournaments per AJGA season</u>. NOTE: Members may compete in a maximum of four Junior All-Star Series tournaments per season (12-15 AGE GROUP).

### *INVITATIONALS & PREVIEW SERIES EVENTS DO NOT COUNT TOWARDS THE FIVE*

## PERFORMANCE BASED ENTRY

<u>Performance Based Entry</u> was introduced in 2003 as the means to determine AJGA tournament fields. This enables members to earn their way into AJGA tournaments based on performances at the national, regional and state levels.

**Members who have already earned Performance Based Entry status should target the following tournaments (others should apply, but be realistic about acceptance):**

If you are under 16, apply to <u>Junior All-Star Series</u> tournaments before each application deadline – applicants who have earned the highest number of Performance Stars will gain entry.

Apply to <u>Open</u> tournaments before each application deadline - applicants who have earned the highest number of Performance Stars will gain entry.

If you are not accepted into the<u> Open or Junior All-Star Series</u> tournament, apply to its associated <u>AJGA Qualifier </u>during the application window to compete for a spot in the tournament field.

# How Entry Into an Open or Junior All-Star Series Tournament Affects Your Status:

## Open Tournaments

Players who are <u>not Fully Exempt</u> that gain entry into an AJGA Open tournament will <u>use 4 earned Performance Stars.</u>

*Example: A player with a status of 10 Performance Stars will drop to six Performance Stars upon entry into an Open tournament.*

Players who gain entry with <u>four or less Performance Stars</u> <u>will use any earned status and drop down to their initial status received for membership</u> (three, two or one Performance Stars).

## Junior All-Star Series Tournament

Players who are <u>not Fully Exempt</u> that gain entry into a Junior All-Star Series Tournament will <u>use 1 earned Performance Star.</u> *Players who gain entry with just their initial status (performance stars received from membership) do not lose their initial status, but do lose priority in the tiebreaker process for future events.*

## Suggestions for New AJGA Members, Non-Members or Members with only a few Stars:

Make sure you only play junior golf tournaments where the winners earn stars.

Play <u>AJGA Open Qualifiers because STARS are awarded</u> — even if you don't qualify for the Tournament (*2 Stars for Top 20% Finish; 1 Star for Top 50% Finish.*)

Our research from 2016 suggest that many times, not every junior who plays a Qualifier plays the actual tournament if he/she qualifies, meaning you do always have to finish near the top to qualify. AJGA Qualifier <u>field size is usually 80 boys and 20 girls</u>. Typically, <u>10 percent</u> of boys and girls in an AJGA Qualifier <u>qualify</u> for the corresponding tournament. The exact number of spots will be posted at AJGA Qualifier registration. In 2015 the <u>average score</u> to qualify into Open tournaments was: Boys - 75.4; Girls - 77.6. The average score to finish in the <u>top 50%</u> of the AJGA Qualifier field and earn a Performance Star was: <u>Boys - 78.3</u>; <u>Girls - 80.6</u>.

Players who <u>apply to AJGA Open or Junior All-Star Series events</u> and <u>do not gain entry</u> are <u>NOT automatically moved</u> to the <u>AJGA Qualifier</u> for that event. They <u>must submit a separate</u> AJGA Qualifier application.

AJGA members should apply for an <u>AJGA Qualifier</u> during the application window which begins the <u>Friday after</u>

the tournament application deadline at 3 pm ET (WHICH IS USUALLY PREVIOUS TUESDAY BY 5 PM) and runs through Monday, Noon ET.

The order applications are received has no effect on the qualifier field. However, players must apply within this window to be considered for the initial field.

AJGA Qualifiers are an excellent opportunity to play the course under tournament conditions and so it is recommended that players in the field participate in the qualifiers as well as a way to gain experience playing the course in tournament conditions.

**There is an Appendix included in the book.
The appendix provides a breakdown of the AJGA
giving players and parent's information on:**

1. **Tournament Qualifying Scores**
2. **Number of Stars to enter each tournament**
3. **Scores to finish top 10 for boys / top 5 for girls**

Please use the resource when you are considering building a schedule keeping in mind what tournaments you can play and what scores will allow you to become a full exempt player. To become a fully exempt player, you need to finish within the top 5 for males in a tournament and top 3 for girls.

## HOME COURSE VS. TOURNAMENT PLAY

The preparation for tournament golf starts at your home facility. Most players with limited experience should understand that whatever you shoot at your home golf course, you should add about 3 shots to what you most likely will shoot in a tournament. This means that if you average 72 at your home course, you can expect to average about 75 at tournaments.

It is also important that the player learn the skill of shooting under par at their home golf course. Like many of the other ideas in this book, shooting under par is a skill and requires practice! Junior golfers are wise to make sure this is a skill they practice often and as they develop should, especially for boys, strive to shoot under par often at their home course. Please note that elite players should be able to shoot 66 or better routinely at their home course.

## WHEN ARE YOU READY TO PLAY TOURNAMENTS?

If I had a son or daughter, I would give them a junior club membership and a float of $250 or so dollars at the beginning of the summer. I would explain to them that, as the infamous Dr. Brian Moore puts it there are 2 types of gambling: responsible and not responsible. Responsible gambling means playing for enough that it gets your attention. For example you might play someone at the club where the loser washes the winner's car or maybe cuts their grass.

I would explain to them that option number one is acceptable and encourage the junior golfer to set up matches. These matches should be between players with similar skills and should focus on 18 holes of stroke play, in which every ball is holed out. This should continue until the player has either reached enough money to pay the entry fee to a tournament or until they are out.

These matches can be great opportunities for the student-athlete to develop skill with limited investment. Likewise for players with fluency issues, matches at the golf course can provide an opportunity to learn to compete and eventually how to win.

My research on the AJGA and NJGS suggest that boys who average better than 75 in tournaments and girls who average better than 78 in tournaments will have no problem earning opportunities to play good tournaments and earn a rank that offers college opportunities. I believe that it is important to know you will shoot in this area before you sign up and play a tournament!

## IMPORTANCE OF WEEKENDS

For the vast majority of junior golfers, weekends are the only times when they have enough time to ensure that they can play 18 holes. Therefore it is extremely important that junior golfers who are serious about college embrace these opportunities and play lots of golf!

*Special Note:* If the junior golfer is not keen to spend a majority of their free time on the golf course and in competition, then it is unlikely that have a strong future in tournament golf.

## JUNIOR GOLFER'S PAR

Par in junior golf is 75. As the research on the AJGA suggests, should you average better than 75, it is highly likely you will play college golf.

## COMPETITION FOR BOYS AND GIRLS

The research of Northwestern professor C. Kirabo Jackson has discovered that girls perform better than boys in a particularly competitive environment. The first evidence of this came from his study of all fifth-graders in the Caribbean nation of Trinidad and Tobago. In this study he found that girls perform better when they attend elite middle schools.

Scott Carrell and James West did a similar experiment at the Air Force Academy, with an all-male population of airmen. They grouped low-performing subjects in squadrons with high-performing subjects, leaving the middle-performers in a separate group. The theory was that the habits of the high-performers would impact and help the low-performers. The problem is that at the end of the semester, more of the at-risk cadets were crumbling, not fewer.

The research suggests that girls and boys interpret competition differently. Girls embrace the opportunity to learn and compete. They see it as an opportunity. Boys see competition as a measure and only want to be associated with winning. Information to the contrary seems to diminish self-esteem and motivation, which results in poorer performance.

## Summary

In this chapter, we have discussed the role of competition in the development of the junior golf. Competition is an important skill for the junior golfer. Like each of the skills discussed in the book, competition requires effort and discipline. The preparation for competition begins long before tournament play with matches at the club. Junior golfers want to be seasoned competitors by the time they play a full tournament schedule.

CHAPTER 6

# The Science of Improvement

———⨳———

*"I cannot teach anybody anything.
I can only make them think"*

*- SOCRATES*

## READING VS RECITING

LET'S START THIS CHAPTER WITH a fun game! Based on the research of Dr. Robert Bjork of UCLA, I would like you to try the following:

Find a book and bookmark two separate passages of a couple of pages in length, some distance apart. Read the two passages (Passage #1 and passage #2), then, sometime later in the day, go back and re-read Passage #1.   Take a break for five minutes then sit down with a pen and a blank piece of paper and turn your thoughts to Passage #2.  Don't re-read it, just jot down what you can remember about it from the first time you read it several hours earlier. Put the text passages and your page of notes away and wait 24 hours. Then sit down with a blank pad and write down as much as you can remember about each of the two passages.

What did you find? Dr. Bjork found that re-reading was a weaker factor in recollection than writing notes was. Why? The harder your brain works to dig out a memory, the greater the increase in your learning.

It is important to understand that these results have been simulated in countless studies, including work on how recitation interacts with memory (A.I. Gates); the effectiveness of intermittent testing during the study-and-learning process (Herbert F. Spitzer); the failure of mere repetition to increase learning (Endel Tulving); and the failure of re-reading to aid in retention (A.A. Callender and M.A. McDaniel).

When applied to golf, I believe it is important that golf practice should feel more difficult than competition. If you feel more pressure on the first tee of a tournament than you do in practice you probably aren't going to be a very good player. The whole idea of practice is to prepare your skills and mental ability so that you can produce under stress. To repeat an important distinction: **It's not a matter of whether you can do it; it's whether you can do it now!** If you work on the range with no real purpose, without feedback, then you will have a very hard time producing consistent results on the golf course.

## GRIT

Noted psychologist Angela Lee Duckworth speaks persuasively on this subject. Duckworth found through exhaustive research that one of the main factors in a young person achieving success is grit. She defined grit as the passion and perseverance necessary to reach long-term goals, plus the stamina to stick with whatever must be done, day in and day out, in some cases for years, so as to make a dream come true. What struck Duckworth during her research was that often, IQ was not the difference between the best and worst students. Some of her stronger students had lower IQs and some students with higher IQ's weren't doing well. As it turned out, the grittier kids, even ones with lower IQ's, usually did better long-term because they weren't deterred by failure and were willing to accept the challenge and continue on.


## Growth Mindset vs Fixed Mindset

Carole Dweck, the Lewis and Virginia Eaton Professor of Psychology at Stanford University, talks about two mindsets, "growth" and "fixed," as strongly influencing how a young person develops scholastically as well as in athletics and other aspects of life. A person with a *growth* mindset demonstrates a love of learning and resilience. He or she visibly enjoys the process and effort of improvement. To this person, obstacles are something to be overcome.

A person with a "fixed" mindset believes that, in activities they have talent or acuity for, things should come easily. In other words, you either can do it or you can't, and nothing much can change that outcome. This type sees obstacles as evidence that they don't have what it takes to achieve. Youngsters with the growth mindset know they need effort to be good at something and effort is what makes you smarter or better at what you do. The growth mindset can be cultivated. As the auto magnate Henry Ford famously said: "Whether you think you can, or think you can't—you're right."

## Chronological and Biological Age

Parents, especially parents of boys, should bear in mind that biological versus chronological age plays an important role in the development of the athlete. It is a simple fact that some boys grow and develop quicker. Progress comes easier because their growth mirrors the timeframes of development, allowing them to maximize potential output (e.g., golf scores). These early developers are going to have an advantage and there is simply nothing that will change that.

In sociology this is termed the "Matthew effect", coined by Robert K. Merton and based on a scriptural passage from the book of Matthew. It reads: "… unto everyone that hath shall be given, and he shall have abundance: but from him that hath not shall be taken even that which he hath." The idea is that early developers earn preferential treatment in opportunities and this provides them with an even bigger advantage.

This point is also demonstrated in Malcolm Gladwell's book, *Outliers*, using a peculiar data point about professional hockey players' birthdays. It turns out that the majority of NHL players are born within the first three months of the calendar year. This makes them up to 11 months older than the boys from their same birth year. In turn, this provides an advantage in development, mentally and physically, which leads to more opportunities to play at a higher level, such as on travel teams. This leads to more practice and better coaching and more playing time.

For parents of athletes it is important to remember that the biological development of your child plays a role in the scholarship process. Should your child experience significant growth after the age of 15, it will likely impact their motor skills and stagnate development. If this occurs, I would suggest you make sure and clarify goals for the student, as well as educate them on how the growth spurt could impact performance in the short term. This conversation will help ensure that goals match up with ability, thus increasing the enjoyment / motivation level of the athlete.

## SUMMARY

This chapter has provided insight by many of the great minds in a number of different areas. In each case, I have provided examples of how their research can help you become a better player. I hope that as you continue to develop as a player you will keep in mind the thoughts presented in this chapter.

# CHAPTER 7

# How Competitive is College Golf

*Sports don't build character; they reveal it*

- *JOHN WOODEN*

## WHO DOES WELL IN COLLEGE GOLF

I BELIEVE THAT COLLEGE GOLF has an important role in the development of the golfer; it allows them to build experience in tournament competition, as well as work on many of the skills needed to play elite golf. These skills include being independent, competitive, self-motivated and being able to bounce back after a poor tournament.

In many cases what college golf does not offer, is the ability to continue to build your technical golf swing. Golfers should be encouraged to invest heavily in their junior career to ensure they have a stable and repetitive swing. This will serve them well in their college days. This advice is contrary to what most parents and students hear. Instead, so many within the junior golf community encourage playing a lot of tournaments to gain exposure and earn a scholarship. In my opinion this is only good advice if you have already spent sufficient time building great ball control. The nature of college golf is so competitive, that if you do not have these skills when you arrive, you are not likely to have the opportunity to improve your skills and you may not play as much as you would like.

For junior golfers late in the process, I would encourage them to think long term about their golf. If you are a junior, you may consider using not only a GAP year but also maybe attending a junior college for a year. This will allow you time to develop the skills necessary to make the best of your time in college.

Special note to guys and girls who love to practice: Make sure in the recruiting process you are very open about this preference. Many coaches like to create "competitive environments" in which they expect players to play a lot (either on the golf course or games in practice). This environment can be very different for someone who loves to practice; they have to be open to making the change. If they are not, then it is likely the result will not be positive.

## SEPTEMBER 1 CONTACT RULE AND ITS IMPACT ON YOU

NCAA coaches are now allowed to contact you as of September 1 of your junior year. In many cases now coaches are communicating with seniors and juniors simultaneously. In the past, we had many examples where coaches would wait, miss on athletes and settle at the last minute. I think now that coaches have the opportunity to recruit early, they are less likely to settle on a senior and more likely to get a junior.

For the junior golfer, if you have not heard from any schools by January to March of your junior year, then it is time to take action by starting to make lists and communicating with schools.

## COMPETITION AND SCHOOL DECISION

Before the college decision, I want to share the story of Caroline Sacks. Caroline's story has been told in the book, *David and Goliath: Underdogs, Misfits, and the Art of Battling Giants*, also by Malcolm Gladwell. A talented student, Ms. Sacks found herself struggling in her senior year to decide whether to attend Brown University or the University of Maryland. Based on brand and prestige, she chose Brown and quickly found that the competition level was much more then she anticipated. Quickly she was unable to compete and gave up her goal of being a scientist.

For parents guiding a student-athlete, it is important to understand their child's selection of a university from a holistic perspective. Of course you will be seeking to identify the best school among all those the student could gain admission to. Further, however, you need to weigh such factors as their maturity, their social skills and their survival skills. Under the latter category are such questions as how well they might adapt to campus life and independence, how responsible are they, how hard are they likely to work at school, how high are the academic standards, and how their success at the school will match their prior success. You should also consider what support systems are in place at each school on their list.

In order for this whole process to be successful, it is important for the parent to mentally separate what they want from what is ultimately best for their student. All parents want the best for their children but for each child this is unique. Some students don't love school, but if you are thoughtful, you can put them in an environment where they can compete, earn good grades, have a great experience, mature and perhaps position themselves for graduate work in the future. On the other hand, a parent can push hard for the better school and have their student select it, only to find that, like Caroline, they get uncomfortable, change majors and put aside dreams. I encourage parents to be thoughtful about the decision and avoid defaulting to the best schools out of hubris.

## JUNIOR COLLEGE

The greatest enjoyment I had as a coach was during my time at Redlands Community College. During my three years I was able to coach and interact with some of the best people and players in the world. For this reason, I would like to suggest that if you are struggling in the recruiting process **CONSIDER JUNIOR COLLEGE!** If you lack experience, strength or size, maturity, money or opportunity (or any combination) it is highly likely that a junior college would be a great option.

## THE NUMBERS GAME

There are about 300 Division I men's and women's golf teams. Let's assume that each of them takes 2.5 players per year for men's golf and two for women's golf (this would mean the average men's team would have 10 players and the average women's team would have eight). By this bit of arithmetic, we see that each year only the top 750 boys and top 600 girls will have a chance to play Division1 golf.

Now let's consider some numbers:

Number of Players on the NJGS
Boys 8600
Girls 2850

According to the European Golf Association Website the number in several northern European Countries are- (http://www.ega-golf.ch/federations)

Belgium – 6,785 junior players
Holland – 16, 333 junior players
Germany – 47,178 junior players
Sweden - 47,333 junior players
Denmark – 8,478 junior players

Obviously these numbers include boys and girls, of which many might not want to play college golf. The point is that golf is an international game with hundreds of thousands of players competing for the opportunity to play here. This means that if you are ranked 750 in NJGS, you are probably closer to No. 1500 in the world. This puts you a lot closer to a D3 or NAIA program than to a high-echelon D1 program.

## STATS: HOW GOOD ARE DIFFERENT PLAYERS?

In 2015 the second-ranked player in The Golfstat Cup standings for women was my friend Tiffany Chan of Daytona State Community College with an average of 70.80. The 20th player, Elsa Westin, was at an NAIA school, Northwood (now Keiser University). Westin averaged 72.08. In men's golf, the 10th best player, Santiago Gomez, was from Nova Southeastern University, a Division II school, and averaged 70.61. In 2016, the Lynn University Division II men's golf team will have three players ranked in the top 500, and two in the top 800 in the WAGR. In the 2015 season opener, Oglethorpe University (a top Division III school) shot minus-13 in a tournament.

The point here is that there are a lot of good players at all levels. If you play at any level in college you needn't worry that you won't see a lot of very good competition. You should never rule out a school because of the label of it—a label that says NAIA, Division III, or community college.

## THE RECRUITING FUNNEL

Let's use the image of a funnel to help explain the recruiting process. At the top of the funnel are some 250 to 500 student-athletes. In the middle are the unofficial visits. This is a tricky number because some schools are open to many visits, especially by local student-athletes or people with ties to the program. This can put the number higher but in general it will be between 15 and 25 unofficial visits per year. Next are the official visits. These will number no higher than six most years. Then at the bottom are the student-athletes who commit and play on the team; normally just two or three, and perhaps just one.

## FORM LETTERS

It is important for student-athletes to understand that many coaches use a vast net early in the recruiting process as a way to hedge against missing on late developers. The way they do this is through what is called a form letter. A form letter is a correspondence that describes the college in depth including facilities, success of alumni, recent results, academics, success of school, rankings of academic or athletic, upcoming events and so forth.

Understanding form letters is important. Coaches are going to start with a group of between 100-400 students who receive these letters on a regular basis (between 1-2 times per week for top programs). ***Should you receive one of these, it does not necessarily mean that you are a top recruit and will get an offer. Instead, it means you are in a large group of students in which the coach is potentially interested***.

## RULE OF THE NO. 1 PLAYER

The No. 1 player rule is something every wise recruiter lives by. The idea is to always be on the recruiting trail in search of someone who can play No. 1 on your team, either immediately or shortly in the future.

## THE SEVEN-YEAR IMPACT

If a great player comes to a college, such as an Oliver Schniederjans at Georgia Tech or a John Rahm at Arizona State, it has roughly a seven-year impact on the program. Not only do these difference-maker players help their teams win, they also help recruit other good players. If as a senior at ASU, John Rahm helps convince a 2016 high school senior, that person will then contribute to the team for another 4 years, making a huge impact on the program.

## THE ROLE OF STARS IN WINNING

According to the book by Mark de Rond, "There Is An I in Team," any team with no starting all-star player has less than a one percent chance of winning the NBA championship. By comparison a team with one all-star enjoys a 7.1 percent chance of winning and a 16 percent chance of making it to the finals. He goes on to say "those with pockets deep enough to field two first-team all-star players have a one-in-four chance of winning a championship and better than a one in three chance of making the finals." He also states that a superstar with a relatively weak supporting cast fares better than a team with five good players.

In college golf, the benchmark for success is the Golfstat Cup. It ranks the top 250 players in both men's and women's golf regardless of division. To de Rond's point, you will find when studying it that here is a strong relationship between the number of top-250 players on a team and the tournament performance of that team.

## SUMMARY

Golf has grown over the last 20 years internationally. Today there are not only more juniors, but juniors who are receiving exceptional coaching. The result is that college golf has become extremely competitive. Junior golfers and their parents need to closely examine all the factors, as well as the other comments in this chapter, to make sure that they are targeting the right group of schools that match their student athlete.

# CHAPTER 8

# What the Student Athlete Needs to Know

**"The greatest enemy of knowledge is not ignorance; it is the illusion of knowledge."**

**- STEPHEN HAWKING**

## FIRST BIG DECISION

FOR THE VAST MAJORITY OF young people, the college decision is their first life major choice. This chapter is designed to expose parents and students too many ideas that can help them make the best possible decision.Life vs. the Four-year Decision

## THE FOUR INPUTS OF THE SCHOLARSHIP PROCESS

It is important that parents and student-athletes understand that coaches look at four main inputs when recruiting — golf, academics, interview and finances.

**Golf**: The three main components for golf are scoring average, head-to-head record and rounds under par. For boys it is very important to have some rounds under par. It is also important to note that coaches will strongly consider head to head over score in situations where the field is strong and conditions are tough.

**Academics**: SAT/ACT, GPA, class rank and high school reputation are the most important factors.

**Interview**: The interview is a critical part of the process and is the biggest reason that students get opportunities, for several reasons. It is important to remember that in Division I golf there are 303 schools. Of these it is likely that only about 10 percent have a chance to win a national championship. This means 90 percent do not. For these coaches, while it is important to compete in their conferences, it is equally as important to have ***really good kids that they like and do not cause problems***! A majority of coaches do not get paid enough to deal with headaches. If during the interview they feel a student (or parent) is high maintenance and not going to make a significant contribution to the program, they could pass on the student-athlete.

**Finances**: As we know from de Rond's research in the last chapter — The Role of Stars in Winning — superstars are tied to the success of teams. To be successful in men's golf, I think coaches need to get two to five players on low scholarships (less than 30 percent) so that they can spend money on super stars, who generally command more than 80 percent.There are 988 men's golf programs in the United States — Division I, Division II, Division III and NAIA — with 729 on the women's side. The  four above inputs determine how many of them you can attend. For example if you are a female golfer with a perfect SAT, unlimited budget and a scoring average of 71, you have all 729 options. On the other hand, if you have a 700 SAT, 1.7 GPA, a $5,000 budget, and a 100 scoring average, you may only have two to four options.

## LIFE V S. THE FOUR-YEAR DECISION

It is important for parents and their student-athlete to discuss the college search process. College plays an important role in a person's development—across the spectrum. College is often where two people meet who will eventually marry. It's where contacts are made that strongly affect career and employment. Obviously, it has a strong effect on intellectual development. As we will see, playing college golf is very competitive. It is also a lot of work and so it is advised that parents educate their children about the options, including simply attending the best academic school to which admission can be gained.

## THE DETAILS OF A VISIT

The coach is very likely to provide you a detailed itinerary for the trip. This should include

- A student host to stay with
- A tour of the campus
- Time with academic support people
- Tour of the golf facilities
- Meeting most or all members of the current team

- Meeting the assistant coach
- Seeing a sporting event on campus
- Time with coaches (possibly a dinner)

It is very important to use your time alone with the players and coach effectively. This is your chance to ask questions and make sure that the school, golf team and coach are a good fit for you.
Some things you may want to accomplish include:

Interviewing the coach:

- What is the coach's philosophy?
- What are the coach's strengths and weaknesses?
- How does the coach interact with other swing coaches?
- How can the coach support you when you turn professional?
- How can the coach support you when you go out looking for a job?

Interviewing the other players about their experience:

- What other schools did you consider?
- What is the best feature of this school? Worst feature?
- How do players get to the course?
- Has the coach ever cut scholarships?
- How does the coach deal with discipline?
- How does the coach conduct qualifying? Is it a fair system?

- How would you describe the players? *(Note: Coaches generally have a particular type of player in mind. Do you fit with these players?)*
- How hard is the school academically? How much support is there?

Understand academics / academic support

- Are tutors available?
- Is there priority registration for athletes?
- How important are academics to the coach?

Dorms

- How is the food?
- Do students feel comfortable in the dorms?
- Who will you live with? Other golfers? Athletes?
- How hard is campus to navigate?
- Parking, etc.

Play at least one of the golf courses

- How do you like it? How does it fit your game? How do your scores compare to average qualifying scores?
- How many other courses are local?
- If there are limited courses, what condition do you expect the course to be in?

## THANK-YOU LETTERS.

Throughout this whole process, maybe one of the most important things you can do is taking the time to hand-write and mail a personal thank-you letter to each coach. Trust me; these go a long way!

## HOW MUCH DO YOU WANT TO PLAY?

A major topic of conversation among coaches, players and parents is playing time. Over the years, I have heard a variety of theories on playing time. Opinions have come from students who want to be the best, who want to play on a competitive team where they are in the middle, and everywhere in between.

In my opinion, the best attribute of college golf is the opportunity for you to test your game in competition against top players 24 days per year (maximum number of tournament days by NCAA Division One rules). I would not be afraid to be the best player on the team because that would make me less likely involved in the "qualifying process." This allows you to focus on improving your game and proper practice to prepare for the tournament.

## EARLY PLAYING DILEMMA

Playing time is an important factor in the decision. With that being said, families and students need to understand that early playing time may be a curse. When the student-athlete is playing golf the first couple weeks of a semester, other students are forming social groups. When the season is finally over and the student has time to socialize, he realizes that many of his classmates have formed groups and are already bonded. Some of these groups will resist new members and often the student-athlete can feel very isolated.

## QUALIFYING

Qualifying for the chance to be one of the official competitors representing your college team in the upcoming tournament is often at the heart of many problems on a team. It should be carefully discussed during the recruiting process. It is critical that the student-athlete understand the basic system of the coach.

Qualifying has many upsides and downside. It encourages competitiveness and rewards players who are able to shoot good scores on command. However it also rewards players who might play their "home" or qualifying course well. It also gives a major advantage to upperclassmen who have a lot of experience playing that particular course (for this reason don't be surprised if you are an upperclassman who ties a freshman in qualifying only to see your coach select the younger player).

I believe the best coaches are going to change qualifying each year based on their squad and variables like the number of great players, experience of the players, tournament schedule (times and gaps) and other duties of the coach (family / personal or administrative). For example, if you have two returning All-Americans on your team, your coach would most likely set up a system where three spots are available for the other members of the team to try for. This allows them to include their All-Americans in the lineup every time.

College golf puts a major premium on playing rather than practicing. Golfers face 24 days of competition on the road (8-12 tournaments) and probably another 4-5 qualifying tournaments within seven months (September – November and February to May). That's 12-17 tournaments in just over half a year. This means that players must show up with the proper fundamental skills, including ball control and ideas on how to practice, in order to be successful.

One year I decided to use the "point system" for qualifying. The system was simple, as I told the members of my team: "If I point to you, you are going to the tournament."

## Team Dynamics in Recruiting

Team Dynamics is an interesting part of the recruiting process. From my experience, it is very important to remember that each year the team is going to be a little different. It is also important to consider the size of the team and the strength of the team and how they interact. Often coaches with smaller teams are going to care a lot more about team chemistry and strongly consider how the players will interact. This may also be a greater consideration among women's coaches and players.

On the best teams in the country, maybe top the 25-30, I think that team chemistry is far less of an issue for coaches. In fact, I have had many experiences in which some of the best teams (and players) don't care at all about their team mates, coaches or chemistry at all! The point is that you should assess the dynamics of the teams you visit and decide if they will be a good fit for your personality and style.

## ACADEMICS VS. ATHLETICS?
It is important for parents and student-athletes in grade 10 to take a serious look at the academic route versus the athletic route to college. If you want to go to an elite academic school, I recommend a goal of 700 on all sections of the SAT and an average golf score of 75 strokes or lower per 18 holes.

If you are trying to be a great golfer and go to a school that turns out tour players, I would suggest a scoring average from 71.5 to 72.5, top-100 WAGR or better and a combined 900 on your SATs. If you want to be an early commit/signee selection, you have to realistically be within the top 100 on the Junior Golf Scoreboard and between 250 and 500 on the WAGR.

The toughest scenario for a high school student-athlete is to be is in the middle, because it is more of a challenge to find a fit. In the middle means you have scored about a 1010 on the SAT and you are a 75 or higher shooter. You are distinct in neither respect and there are hundreds, if not thousands, of people like you. In this situation, it is best to send emails that lead off with your best quality. This could be a great golf swing or maybe steady improvement in golf scores over the prior two years or even a story about being new to the game. There are some programs that are intrigued by these types of players. The key is to successfully discover them, so don't be afraid to send out a lot of emails!

Once you have chosen between academics and athletics as your path, have that be reflected in the way you set up your communications, whether via email or other methods. If you are trying for entry into a top academic school, put your GPA and test scores very early in the email, perhaps even in the subject line. This is important because although there is great interest in the leading academic schools among top junior golfers, most of these potential applicants do not meet the requirements. By meeting the requirements, you open up the opportunity to be recruited. If your strength is your golf scores, and you're going the athletics path, communicate on that basis. You may want to lead with your ranking (WAGR, NJGS or Golfweek) or scoring average. You probably want to follow this with a swing video and some information about your practice schedule or development plan.

## I'M ONLY COMING FOR GOLF

Over the years I have heard a lot of players, especially international students, who struggle, say that the only reason they want to attend school is because of golf. In fact, almost 20 years ago, I was one of those students. Looking back, I would say that I misunderstood the amount of experience I would get through the college process. School is an important part of the process, including those dreaded general education classes (my least favorite was music appreciation), however you should gain a lot of other experiences at college. Don't undervalue these experiences as part of your development towards your goals.

The other problem with this thinking, is that during the decision making process you might tend to hone in on one to three things. For example, for me, Campbell was a great experience because it had 36 holes of golf on campus in nice weather. However it was not a fit intellectually, spiritually, socially or for the coach. As a result when golf was going bad, I had no connection to the school and was 100% completely miserable.

The best time to get this experience is during a visit. My advice is to never commit to a school without doing the following:

1.  Stay in the dorms and spend time with your team mates
2.  Spend time alone with the coach and have a specific talk about what they will do in your personal development
3.  Have your personal coach and college golf coach connect
4.  Spend time in a class, eat in the cafeteria and see the campus in different weather. For example, if you are from the North and thinking about University of Central Florida, see the campus in August when the temperature is the hottest. Likewise, if you are not accustomed

to cold weather and thinking about a northern school go visit in January or February.

## Considerations for the Potential Walk-On

Many players have dreams of playing at major conference schools. With demand, coaches some times are able to get very competitive players on lower scholarships that range from 1-30%. The player must carefully weigh the options and factors like playing time, facilities, school experience and finances.

## What to Expect as a Walk-On

Here are some things to expect as a walk on –

1. Better players with more experience getting more playing time. Scholarships are usually award to players with the best record over long periods of time. Just because you may beat this player by a couple shots in qualifying does not always mean you will play.
2. Seniors are a lot physically stronger then freshman (most of the time)
3. Upperclassmen have a significant advantage in knowing the "home" course
4. Having a strong relationship with the coach is important. If you are going to walk on, make it a priority to go to the coaches office often and spend time with them

SUMMARY

For the student athlete, the college decision is more complex because they are looking to maximize their options for both academics and athletics. In this chapter, we have spoken about key ideas in the process including playing time, asking good questions and academic vs athletic fit. I hope you will consider each of these as you move forward in your decision.

# CHAPTER 9

# The Basics of College Golf Scholarships

―――⟨∞⟩―――

**"If you don't know where you are going,
you might wind up someplace else."**

- YOGI BERRA

## THE NCAA

THE NCAA, OR NATIONAL COLLEGIATE Athletic Association, was established in 1906 and serves as the athletics governing body for more than 1,300 colleges, universities, conferences and organizations. The national office is in Indianapolis, Indiana, but the member colleges and universities develop the rules and guidelines for athletics eligibility and athletics competition for each of the three NCAA divisions. The NCAA is committed to the student-athlete and to governing competition in a fair, safe, inclusive and sportsmanlike manner.

The NCAA membership includes:

* 346 active Division I members;
* 298 active Division II members; and
* 440 active Division III members.

One of the differences among the three divisions is that colleges and universities in Divisions I and II may offer athletic scholarships. Division III colleges and universities do not.

Information about NCAA eligibility can be found on the NCAA website at http://ncaa.org.

## Schools that Sponsor Golf

Within the NCAA, there are 813 men's programs and 566 women's programs:

* Division 1:  303 Men's and 264 Women's program
* Division 2:  224 Men's and 166 Women's programs
* Division 3:  286 Men's and 136 Women's programs

## What is the NAIA?

The National Association of Intercollegiate Athletics (NAIA) is an independent league of colleges and universities that offer students an opportunity to engage in sports. The leagues' governing body, like the NCAA, oversees the rules and regulations regarding student-athletes in areas such as scholarship, eligibility, amateurism, travel and much more. Going into the 2016-2017 season, the NAIA has 175 men's golf teams and 163 women's golf teams.

## NAIA ELIGIBILITY

To be eligible in the NAIA you must meet two of the following three criteria:

1. 860 on the Math and reading sections of the SAT
2. 2.0 GPA
3. Graduate in the top half of your class – verification of this to come via letter from your school administration

## WHAT IS THE NJCAA?

The National Junior College Athletic Association is the governing body of Junior College or two-year schools (according to Golfstat, 62 men's golf programs; 21 women's golf programs). These schools deserve note in this book because I believe they are very strong options for many families, particularly if you believe your student-athlete needs the following:

1. A smaller environment to help build skills academically, athletically, socially and help with overall maturity
2. Time to develop (Son or daughter has a young biological age)
3. You want to go to a larger university but don't have the offers

4.  Finances are an issues (these schools typically cost less than $15,000 for everything

## NUMBER OF SCHOLARSHIPS AVAILABLE

Special Note – The NCAA defines a full scholarship as tuition, fees, room and board and course related text books.

*Shown below are the numbers of scholarships allowed:*

**Men's Golf**
NCAA DI: 4.5
NCAA DII: 3.6
NAIA: 5
NJCAA: 8

**Women's Golf**
NCAA DI: 6
NCAA DII: 5.4
NAIA: 5
NJCAA: 8

## FUNDED VS NON-FUNDED

Based on direct experience, I would estimate that 50 percent of these men's programs are fully funded and 65 percent of the women's programs are. "Fully funded" is technically defined as having the ability to offer the full amount of scholarship under the NCAA rules.

Many people make their decisions based on the label of the division. I find this to be shortsighted, because the worth of a program has less to do with division and more to do with the commitment of the administration, donors and greater community. For example the Division 2 powerhouse Nova Southeastern University boasts their own golf course, 27,000 students and the perfect weather of South Florida.  .

    I would therefore recommend that student-athletes look at schools in terms of two pools, funded versus non-funded. Funded programs can be defined as any program that has put a strong financial commitment towards golf.

## IN-STATE ACADEMIC SCHOLARSHIPS

Several states offer academic scholarships geared towards encouraging students to attend school in their home state. In Florida and Georgia these are called Bright Futures and Hope, respectively. In the recruiting process, athletes need to understand that these scholarships offer a subsidy to the university athletic program. College golf coaches find they can recruit in-state players at a great discount. This, along with the relative quality of in-state talent, makes spots at schools in these states not only competitive athletically, but also financially. It's something to keep in mind as you look from one state to the next for the schools you'll consider.

## TOEFL

TOEFL or Test of English as a foreign language is one of the admissions requirements for many international students whose first language is not English. This test is often over looked by international students, however I want to warn you that it is very challenging! Parents and students are well advised to make it a priority and ensure by the start of senior year that the minimum score has been met.

## SUMMARY

This chapter has been an opportunity to learn about the NCAA and NAIA, including the number of scholarship available through each. We have also discussed different resources you should use in the process including Golfstat; the College-Bound Student Athlete; and the College Board. Each will help you gain valuable insight into college's academics and athletics. Finally, I have introduced you to the idea of looking at programs as funded or non-funded. I think this is a unique way toevaluate schools and ensure students will enroll in a program that provides them the resources to improve.

CHAPTER 10

# Information to Guide Your Decision

**"Let yourself be silently drawn by the strange pull of what you really love. It will not lead you astray."**

**- RUMI**

## PARENTS ROLE

I WOULD LIKE TO SPEAK to the parent's role in the process. For me, their role in guiding their son/daughter depends greatly on their ability to view the process as an important opportunity for their child to grow and develop. In my experience, parents often become too attached to the process from a personal perspective and start having an agenda. For example, parents might want the student to attend a certain school that has a prestigious name but they do not realistically assess whether their student has the academic or athletic requirements to be successful in that environment. The process should be about finding their student a place to succeed; to get a great education, deepen their passion for education, connect with new ideas/people and feel confident to be a contributing member of society.

## CULTURE

The culture is going to be unique at each school based on a number of different factors such as the size of school, its location and its affiliation with any religious groups. I would encourage families to have a serious talk about their expectations when it comes to these variables.

I am a graduate of Campbell University in central North Carolina. As a middle-class Canadian who attended public high school in Ontario, I was unfamiliar with the culture I discovered at Campbell, a Baptist-affiliated university. It was a surprise to me to see how many students walked around campus carrying Bibles and to notice how deeply religious people were. I was a little shocked and disoriented by it. One day I saw a sign for a party that was offering free food. There was nothing else on the sign except an address and "BYOB." I hurried out, bought a 24-pack of beer and drove to the address on the sign. When I walked in, I felt all eyes on me and my suitcase of beer. I hadn't known that BYOB at Campbell meant "bring your own bible."

## THE LAW OF ATTRACTION

As a coach I was always interested to see who became friendly with whom during the visit, and during the first couple weeks of school. Over a decade of coaching, I noticed that good players tend to attract each other, and that problem students tend to flock together, as well.

For the student-athlete it is very important to assess who at the school is likely to make up their "golf team social group." Remember that it is highly unlikely for freshman (or underclassmen) to hang out with seniors; therefore your group is probably the current freshman. During the visit it is important to assess their goals and personality as it relates to the student athlete. The closer the match you have in those areas, the better.

## THE NORTHEAST PARADOX

There are many stories from around the country, but particularly in the Northeast, about average students who get into elite schools thanks to their ability to play sports. I am here to tell you that if you want to use a sport to help in your application, then golf is not the sport you should choose. Sports like Basketball, Football, Hockey or Lacrosse are more likely to help in this regard.

## WHAT CAN YOU LIVE WITH?

I have visited over 700 campuses. That experience has taught me that every school has a lot of positive factors. However most of them have at least one, or perhaps two, characteristics that are not ideal. These include everything from location to practice facilities to playing time to coaching to quality of education. It is important that during the visit the student-athlete and family identify the downside of each potential school and then discuss them.

It is extremely likely that after you make your decision, you will feel some level of buyer's remorse. Buyer's remorse is fueled by the feeling that you are missing out on something. *The problem is that no school is perfect, so no matter where you go there will most likely be a downside or two. You should make sure you are aware of these negatives before you make the commitment and that they are things you know you can live with! This is a crucially important point.*


## SHOULD YOU GET HELP IN THE PROCESS?

The Binmore Continuum (created by Richard Thaler of the University of Chicago) is the idea that we do small things often enough to learn how to get them right, but when we get to larger things, such as buying a home, setting up a mortgage, or getting a job, we don't have much practice at those activities or much opportunity to learn about them, and thus we may not do them so well. This theory also applies to the college scholarship process and why you might want to consider getting assistance in making the right choice. It is the reason that I have developed a business focused on helping families like you connect with schools that meet your athletic, academic, social and financial needs.

Thank you for taking time to read this book. I hope that through the book, you have been exposed to many of the key concepts necessary to build skill and ultimately improve your tournament scores to earn an opportunity to play college golf. Should you have any questions about the information in this book, or want further assistance in the process, I would encourage you to reach out to me. I can be reached via my email at Brendan@golfplacementservices.com.

# APPENDIX

The appendix provides a breakdown of the AJGA giving players and parent's information on:

1. Tournament Qualifying Scores
2. Number of Stars to enter each tournament
3. Scores to finish top 10 for boys / top 5 for girls

**\*PLEASE NOTE THAT TOP 10 IS THE SCORING RANGE TO FINISH INSIDE THE TOP 10 AT EACH TOURNAMENT**

**BOYS**

**AJGA Preview at Cypress Ridge**
Boys initial tournament field: ***All members*** with 0 tournament opportunities gained entry.
TOP 10: 144-150

## AJGA Preview at River Ridge
Boys initial tournament field: ***All 2016, 2017, 2018, and 2019*** graduates with 0 tournament opportunities gained entry. ***Twelve 2020*** graduates with 0 tournament opportunities gained entry via tiebreaker.
TOP 10: 144-150

## AJGA Preview at Cimarron Hills
Boys initial tournament field: ***All 2017, 2018, and 2019*** graduates with 0 tournament opportunities gained entry. ***Nine 2020*** graduates with 0 tournament opportunities gained entry via tiebreaker.
TOP 10: 150-154

## AJGA Preview at Carolina Trace
Boys initial tournament field: ***All 2016, 2017, 2018, and 2019*** graduates with 0 tournament opportunities gained entry. ***Three 2020*** graduates with 0 tournament opportunities gained entry via tiebreaker.
TOP 10: 146-155

## AJGA Preview at Ocala
Boys initial tournament field: ***All 2016, 2017, and 2018*** graduates with 0 tournament opportunities gained entry. ***Three 2019*** graduates with 0 tournament opportunities gained entry via tiebreaker.
TOP 10: 145-151

## AJGA Preview at Château Élan presented by Halski Systems

Boys initial tournament field: ***All 2016, 2017, and 2018*** graduates with 0 tournament opportunities gained entry. ***Two 2019*** graduates with 0 tournament opportunities gained entry via tiebreaker.

TOP 10: 140-146

## AJGA Preview at The Glen Club

Boys initial tournament field: ***All 2016 & 2017*** graduates with 0 tournament opportunities gained entry. ***Thirty-one 2018*** graduates with 0 tournament opportunities gained entry via tiebreaker.

TOP 10: 147-154

## AJGA Preview at Dauphin Highlands

Boys initial tournament field: ***All 2016 & 2017*** graduates with 0 tournament opportunities gained entry. ***Twenty-six 2018*** graduates with 0 tournament opportunities gained entry via tiebreaker.

TOP 10: 142-148

## AJGA Preview at Worthington Manor

Boys initial tournament field: ***All 2016 & 2017*** graduates with 0 tournament opportunities gained entry. ***Twenty-six 2018*** graduates with 0 tournament opportunities gained entry via tiebreaker.

TOP 10: 151-156

## AJGA Preview at Sugar Valley

Boys initial tournament field: ***All 2016 & 2017*** graduates with 0 tournament opportunities gained entry. ***Twenty-four 2018*** graduates with 0 tournament opportunities gained entry via tiebreaker.

TOP 10: 143-153

## AJGA Preview at Brookhaven

Boys initial tournament field: ***All 2016 & 2017*** graduates with 0 tournament opportunities gained entry. ***Twenty 2018*** graduates with 0 tournament opportunities gained entry via tiebreaker.

TOP 10: 143-153

## AJGA Preview at Innlsbruck

Boys initial tournament field: ***All 2016 & 2017*** graduates with 0 tournament opportunities gained entry. ***Seventeen 2018*** graduates with 0 tournament opportunities gained entry via tiebreaker.

TOP 10: 143-152

## AJGA Preview at Morongo (Ages 12-15)

Boys initial tournament field: ***All 2018 & 2019*** graduates with 0 tournament opportunities gained entry. ***Two 2020*** graduates with 0 tournament opportunities gained entry via tiebreaker.

TOP 10: 145-153

## AJGA Preview at Innisbrook (Ages 12-15)

Boys initial tournament field: ***All 2018*** graduates with 0 tournament opportunities gained entry. ***Thirty 2019*** graduates with 0 tournament opportunities gained entry via tiebreaker.

TOP 10: 141-154

# BOYS JUNIOR ALL-STAR (AGES 12-15)

## *LISTED EASIEST TO HARDEST*

### AJGA Junior All-Star at Mooring

Boys initial tournament field : All Boys who applied gained entry
TOP 10: 208-227

### Cameron McCormick Junior All-Star

Boys initial tournament field required a status of **_2_** Performance Stars or more to gain entry; **_18_** Boys with **_1_** Performance Star gained entry via PBE tiebreaker.
TOP 10: 204-211

### AJGA Junior All-Star at Spring Valley

Boys initial tournament field required a status of **_2_** Performance Stars or more to gain entry; **_16_** Boys with **_1_** Performance Star gained entry via PBE tiebreaker.
QUALIFIER: 3SCORES THAT QUALIFED =77-78-79
TOP 10: (219-223)

### AJGA Junior All-Star at Lost Springs presented by Visit Bentonville

Boys initial tournament field required a status of **_2_** Performance Stars or more to gain entry; **_13_** Boys with **_1_** Performance Star gained entry via PBE tiebreaker.
TOP 10: 214-218

## Windham Mountain Resort Junior All-Star

Boys initial tournament field required a status of **2** Performance Stars or more to gain entry; **7** Boys with **1** Performance Star gained entry via PBE tiebreaker.

QUALIFIER: 5 SCORES THAT QUALIFED ARE BETWEEN =75-78

TOP 10: 206-218

## Mill Creek Foundation Junior All-Star

Boys initial tournament field required a status of **2** Performance Stars or more to gain entry; **7** Boys with **1** Performance Star gained entry via PBE tiebreaker.

QUALIFIER: 5 SCORES THAT QUALIFIED ARE BETWEEN =73-75

TOP 10: 202-215

## AJGA Junior All-Star at Rush Creek

Boys initial tournament field required a status of **2** Performance Stars or more to gain entry; **2** Boys with **1** Performance Star gained entry via PBE tiebreaker.

QUALIFIER: 2 SCORES OF 72

TOP 10: 204-219

## AJGA Junior All-Star at Diablo Grande

Boys initial tournament field required a status of **3** Performance Stars or more to gain entry; **15** Boys with **2** Performance Stars gained entry via PBE tiebreaker.

QUALIFIER: 6 SCORES BETWEEN =75-82

TOP 10: 210-221

## AJGA Junior All-Star at Chantilly National

Boys initial tournament field required a status of **4** Performance Stars or more to gain entry; **7** Boys with **3** Performance Stars gained entry via PBE tiebreaker.

QUALIFIER: 11 SCORES BETWEEN =71-77

Top 10: 210-218

## AJGA Junior All-Star at Bentwater

Boys initial tournament field required a status of **6** Performance Stars or more to gain entry; **4** Boys with **5** Performance Stars gained entry via PBE tiebreaker.

Top 10: 145-148

## AJGA Junior All-Star at Forsgate presented by the Spinnaker Foundation

Boys initial tournament field required a status of **6** Performance Stars or more to gain entry; **3** Boys with **5** Performance Stars gained entry via PBE tiebreaker.

Top 10: 139-150

## Evitt Foundation RTC Junior All-Star

Boys initial tournament field required a status of **6** Performance Stars or more to gain entry; **1** Boy with **5** Performance Stars gained entry via PBE tiebreaker.

QUALIFIER: 8 SCORES BETWEEN =70-73

Top 10: 199-212

## AJGA Junior All-Star at The Virtues

Boys initial tournament field required a status of **_7_** Performance Stars or more to gain entry; **_7_** Boys with **_6_** Performance Stars gained entry via PBE tiebreaker.
<u>Top 10</u>: 141-147

## Core Golf Academy Junior All-Star

Boys initial tournament field required a status of **_7_** Performance Stars or more to gain entry; **_4_** Boys with **_6_** Performance Stars gained entry via PBE tiebreaker.
<u>QUALIFIER</u>: 8 SCORES BETWEEN 72-75
<u>Top 10</u>: 211-221

## AJGA Junior All-Star at El Conquistador

Boys initial tournament field required a status of **_8_** Performance Stars or more to gain entry; **_4_** Boys with **_7_** Performance Stars gained entry via PBE tiebreaker.
<u>Top 10</u>: 216-223

# BOYS OPEN TOURNAMENT (AGES 12-18)

# #1 LEVEL (1-9 STARS)

*<u>EASIEST ONES TO GET INTO, IN DESCENDING ORDER</u>*
## AJGA Junior at Centennial

Boys initial tournament field required a status of **_3_** Performance Stars or more to gain entry; **_5_** Boys with **_2_** Performance Stars gained entry via PBE tiebreaker.

QUALIFIER: 15 SCORES BETWEEN =69-73
TOP 5: 206-210; Top 10: 211-212

## AJGA Junior at Oak Tree

Boys initial tournament field required a status of **_4_** Performance Stars or more to gain entry; **_20_** Boys with **_3_** Performance Stars gained entry via PBE tiebreaker.
QUALIFIER: 10 SCORES BETWEEN =70-74
TOP 5: 196-208; Top 10: 209-212

## Sunriver Junior Open

Boys initial tournament field required a status of **_4_** Performance Stars or more to gain entry; **_14_** Boys with **_3_** Performance Stars gained entry via PBE tiebreaker.
QUALIFIER: 4 SCORES BETWEEN =71-75
TOP 5: 199-213; Top 10: 214-215

## AJGA Kansas Junior at Buffalo Dunes

Boys initial tournament field required a status of **_4_** Performance Stars or more to gain entry; **_7_** Boys with **_3_** Performance Stars gained entry via PBE tiebreaker.
QUALIFIER: 5 SCORES BETWEEN =73-80
TOP 5: 219-223; Top 10: 224-225

## Under Armour® Canadian Championship

Boys initial tournament field required a status of **_4_** Performance Stars or more to gain entry; **_3_** Boys with **_3_** Performance Stars gained entry via PBE tiebreaker.
QUALIFIER: 11 SCORES BETWEEN =70-78
TOP 5: 211-215; Top 10: 216-220

## Coca-Cola Junior Championship at Boyne Highlands

Boys initial tournament field required a status of **4** Performance Stars or more to gain entry.

QUALIFIER: 10 SCORES BETWEEN =71-76

TOP 5: 209-215; Top 10: 216-219

## ACDS / Ryan Moore Junior at Oakbrook

Boys initial tournament field required a status of **4** Performance Stars or more to gain entry.

QUALIFIER: 6 SCORES BETWEEN =71-77

TOP 5: 210-214; Top 10: 216-217

## Killington Junior Golf Championship

Boys initial tournament field required a status of **5** Performance Stars or more to gain entry; **9** Boys with **4** Performance Stars gained entry via PBE tiebreaker.

QUALIFIER: 12 SCORES BETWEEN =69-75

TOP 5: 211-214; Top 10: 215-219

## Lockton Kansas City Junior

Boys initial tournament field required a status of **5** Performance Stars or more to gain entry; **9** Boys with **4** Performance Stars gained entry via PBE tiebreaker.

QUALIFIER: 10 SCORES BETWEEN =71-78

TOP 5: 216-222; Top 10: 223-224

## AJGA City of London Junior Championship

Boys initial tournament field required a status of **5** Performance Stars or more to gain entry; **4** Boys with **4** Performance Stars gained entry via PBE tiebreaker.

QUALIFIER: 15 SCORES BETWEEN =69-76
TOP 5: 203-209; Top 10: 210-215

## Action Zone / Bob Estes Abilene Junior
Boys initial tournament field required a status of **5** Performance Stars or more to gain entry; **4** Boys with **4** Performance Stars gained entry via PBE tiebreaker.
QUALIFIER: 12 SCORES BETWEEN =71-77
TOP 5: (207-216); Top 10: (217-219)

## New Era Junior Championship
Boys initial tournament field required a status of **5** Performance Stars or more to gain entry.
QUALIFIER: 12 SCORES BETWEEN =71-76
TOP 5: (212-216); Top 10: (218-219)

## AJGA Junior at The Legends
Boys initial tournament field required a status of **6** Performance Stars or more to gain entry; **9** Boys with **5** Performance Stars gained entry via PBE tiebreaker.
QUALIFIER: 10 SCORES BETWEEN =72-79
TOP 5: (215-217); Top 10: (218-220)

## the Memorial Junior presented by Ohio Christian University
Boys initial tournament field required a status of **6** Performance Stars or more to gain entry; **9** Boys with **5** Performance Stars gained entry via PBE tiebreaker.
QUALIFIER: 10 SCORES BETWEEN =68-74
TOP 5: (208-214); Top 10: (215)

## Otter Creek Junior Championship
Boys initial tournament field required a status of **6** Performance Stars or more to gain entry; **4** Boys with **5** Performance Stars gained entry via PBE tiebreaker.
QUALIFIER: 19 SCORES BETWEEN =72-78
TOP 5: (205-212); Top 10: (213-214)

## AJGA Junior at The Ranch
Boys initial tournament field required a status of **6** Performance Stars or more to gain entry; **3** Boys with **5** Performance Stars gained entry via PBE tiebreaker.
QUALIFIER: 11 SCORES BETWEEN =72-77
TOP 5: (204-219); Top 10: (220-222)

## Natural Resource Partners Bluegrass Junior hosted by J.B. Holmes
Boys initial tournament field required a status of **6** Performance Stars or more to gain entry.
QUALIFIER: 13 SCORES BETWEEN =69-74
TOP 5: (202-208); Top 10: (209-210)

## AJGA Shanshan Feng Junior Championship
Boys initial tournament field required a status of **7** Performance Stars or more to gain entry; **10** Boys with **6** Performance Stars gained entry via PBE tiebreaker.
QUALIFIER: 14 SCORES BETWEEN =68-79
TOP 5: (210-219); Top 10: (220-223)

## Randy Wise Junior Open

Boys initial tournament field required a status of **7** Performance Stars or more to gain entry; **4** Boys with **6** Performance Stars gained entry via PBE tiebreaker.

QUALIFIER: 12 SCORES BETWEEN =68-74

TOP 5: (209-218); Top 10: (220-222)

## AJGA Reno / Tahoe Junior at ArrowCreek

Boys initial tournament field required a status of **7** Performance Stars or more to gain entry; **3** Boys with **6** Performance Stars gained entry via PBE tiebreaker.

QUALIFIER: 11 SCORES BETWEEN =73-76

TOP 5: 219-221; Top 10: 223-226

## St. Francisville Area Foundation Junior at The Bluffs

Boys initial tournament field required a status of **7** Performance Stars or more to gain entry; **3** Boys with **6** Performance Stars gained entry via PBE tiebreaker.

QUALIFIER: 12 SCORES BETWEEN =73-78

TOP 5: 221-224; Top 10: 225-228

## FORE Performance Junior Championship

Boys initial tournament field required a status of **7** Performance Stars or more to gain entry; **2** Boys with **6** Performance Stars gained entry via PBE tiebreaker.

QUALIFIER: 11 SCORES BETWEEN =71-77

TOP 5: 213-221; Top 10: 224-227

## David Toms Foundation Shreveport Junior

Boys initial tournament field required a status of **7** Performance Stars or more to gain entry; **2** Boys with **6** Performance Stars gained entry via PBE tiebreaker.

QUALIFIER: 7 SCORES BETWEEN =73-76

TOP 5: 208-216; Top 10: 217-219

## AJGA Junior at Owensboro

Boys initial tournament field required a status of **7** Performance Stars or more to gain entry; **1** Boy with **6** Performance Stars gained entry via PBE tiebreaker.

QUALIFIER: 12 SCORES BETWEEN =70-74

TOP 5: 206-212; Top 10: 213-214

## Wincraft / McArthur Towel & Sports Future Legends

Boys initial tournament field required a status of **8** Performance Stars or more to gain entry; **5** Boys with **7** Performance Stars gained entry via PBE tiebreaker.

QUALIFIER: 11 SCORES BETWEEN =71-76

TOP 5: 220-223; Top 10: 224-227

Under Armour® / Gary Woodland Championship
Boys initial tournament field required a status of **8** Performance Stars or more to gain entry; **5** Boys with **7** Performance Stars gained entry via PBE tiebreaker.

QUALIFIER: 9 SCORES BETWEEN =73-79

TOP 5: 216-224; Top 10: 225-226

## AJGA Junior at Forest Lake presented by Tom Holzer Ford

Boys initial tournament field required a status of **_8_** Performance Stars or more to gain entry; **_1_** Boy with **_7_** Performance Stars gained entry via PBE tiebreaker.
QUALIFIER: 15 SCORES BETWEEN =68-71
TOP 5: 207-215; Top 10: 216

## AJGA Huntsville Junior

Boys initial tournament field required a status of **_8_** Performance Stars or more to gain entry; **_1_** Boy with **_7_** Performance Stars gained entry via PBE tiebreaker.
QUALIFIER: 12 SCORES BETWEEN =69-72
TOP 5: 212-218; Top 10: 220-221

## AJGA Hale Irwin Colorado Junior presented by Huntington Industrial Partners

Boys initial tournament field required a status of **_8_** Performance Stars or more to gain entry; **_1_** Boy with **_7_** Performance Stars gained entry via PBE tiebreaker.
QUALIFIER: 5 SCORES BETWEEN =71-72
TOP 5: 206-209; Top 10: 210-214

## Judie Oppenheimer Memorial Junior

Boys initial tournament field required a status of **_9_** Performance Stars or more to gain entry; **_3_** Boys with **_8_** Performance Stars gained entry via PBE tiebreaker.
QUALIFIER: 14 SCORES BETWEEN =70-77
TOP 5: 215-223; Top 10: 224

## Junior Golf Hub Championship
Boys initial tournament field required a status of **9** Performance Stars or more to gain entry; **2** Boys with **8** Performance Stars gained entry via PBE tiebreaker.
QUALIFIER: 12 SCORES BETWEEN =72-76
TOP 5: 209-211; Top 10: 212-213

## AJGA Junior at Cattail Creek
Boys initial tournament field required a status of **9** Performance Stars or more to gain entry; **1** Boy with **8** Performance Stars gained entry via PBE tiebreaker.
QUALIFIER: 13 SCORES BETWEEN =69-73
TOP 5: 209-215; Top 10: 216-218

## EaglesDream Golf Academy Junior Open
Boys initial tournament field required a status of **9** Performance Stars or more to gain entry.
QUALIFIER: 10 SCORES BETWEEN =70-74
TOP 5: 210-216; Top 10: 217-218

# #2 LEVEL (10-19 STARS)

*EASIEST ONES TO GET INTO, IN DESCENDING ORDER*
## AJGA / CJGT Junior at Yorba Linda
Boys initial tournament field required a status of **10** Performance Stars or more to gain entry; **4** Boys with **9** Performance Stars gained entry via PBE tiebreaker.
TOP 5: 210-214; Top 10: 215-216

## Lessing's AJGA Classic

Boys initial tournament field required a status of **_10_** Performance Stars or more to gain entry.
QUALIFIER: 13 SCORES BETWEEN =67-74
TOP 5: 209-212; Top 10: 213-215

## Greg Norman Champions Golf Academy Junior Championship

Boys initial tournament field required a status of **_11_** Performance Stars or more to gain entry; **_3_** Boys with **_10_** Performance Stars gained entry via PBE tiebreaker.
QUALIFIER: 14 SCORES BETWEEN =70-77
TOP 5: 213-220; Top 10: 221-222

## E-Z-GO Vaughn Taylor Championship presented by PotashCorp

Boys initial tournament field required a status of **_11_** Performance Stars or more to gain entry; **_2_** Boys with **_10_** Performance Stars gained entry via PBE tiebreaker.
QUALIFIER: 10 SCORES BETWEEN =73-76
TOP 5: 213-220; Top 10: 221-223

## Bass Pro Shops / Payne Stewart Junior Championship

Boys initial tournament field required a status of **_11_** Performance Stars or more to gain entry; **_1_** Boy with **_9_** Performance Stars, the next highest status level, gained entry via PBE tiebreaker.
TOP 5: 209-212; Top 10: 214-216

## PING Phoenix Junior at ASU Karsten

Boys initial tournament field required a status of **_12_** Performance Stars or more to gain entry.
QUALIFIER: 8 SCORES BETWEEN =70-73
TOP 5: 195-211; Top 10: 212-213

## Valero Junior Texas Open

Boys initial tournament field required a status of _**13**_ Performance Stars or more to gain entry; _**3**_ Boys with _**12**_ Performance Stars gained entry via PBE tiebreaker.
QUALIFIER: 15 SCORES BETWEEN =66-71
TOP 5: 226-231; Top 10: 232

## Ryan Moore Junior Championship at Anthem

Boys initial tournament field required a status of _**15**_ Performance Stars or more to gain entry; _**2**_ Boys with _**13**_ Performance Stars, the next highest status level, gained entry via PBE tiebreaker.
QUALIFIER: 8 SCORES BETWEEN =69-72
TOP 5: 210-218; Top 10: 219-220

Under Armour® / Scott Stallings Championship presented by Pilot Flying J
Boys initial tournament field required a status of _**15**_ Performance Stars or more to gain entry; _**2**_ Boys with _**14**_ Performance Stars gained entry via PBE tiebreaker.
QUALIFIER: 9 SCORES BETWEEN =67-72
TOP 5: 205-206; Top 10: 208-210

## Daniel Berger Junior Championship

Boys initial tournament field required a status of _**16**_ Performance Stars or more to gain entry; _**1**_ Boy with _**15**_ Performance Stars gained entry via PBE tiebreaker.
QUALIFIER: 12 SCORES BETWEEN =73-80
TOP 5: 210-218; Top 10: 219-224

## Enagic Junior Championship

Boys initial tournament field required a status of **_17_** Performance Stars or more to gain entry; **_5_** Boys with **_16_** Performance Stars gained entry via PBE tiebreaker.
QUALIFIER: 10 SCORES BETWEEN =70-73
TOP 5: 205-209; Top 10: 210-212

## Under Armour® / Alison Lee Championship

Boys initial tournament field required a status of **_17_** Performance Stars or more to gain entry; **_2_** Boys with **_16_** Performance Stars gained entry via PBE tiebreaker.
QUALIFIER: 17 SCORES BETWEEN =73-78
TOP 5: 214-218; Top 10: 219-220

## AJGA Junior at Carlton Oaks

Boys initial tournament field required a status of **_17_** Performance Stars or more to gain entry.
TOP 5: 138-143; Top 10: 145-147

## Rome Junior Classic presented by State Mutual Insurance Company

Boys initial tournament field required a status of **_18_** Performance Stars or more to gain entry; **_4_** Boys with **_17_** Performance Stars gained entry via PBE tiebreaker.
TOP 5: 133-141; Top 10: 143

## IZOD AJGA Championship

Boys initial tournament field required a status of **_18_** Performance Stars or more to gain entry; **_1_** Boy with **_17_** Performance Stars gained entry via PBE tiebreaker.

QUALIFIER: 12 SCORES BETWEEN =68-70
TOP 5: 203-209; Top 10: 210-215

## AJGA Philadelphia Junior

Boys initial tournament field required a status of **_18_** Performance Stars or more to gain entry.
QUALIFIER: 12 SCORES BETWEEN =70-74
TOP 5: 211-217; Top 10: 218-220

## Insperity Invitational / Patrick Reed AJGA Junior Championship presented by Callaway Golf

Boys initial tournament field required a status of **_19_** Performance Stars or more to gain entry.
QUALIFIER: 10 SCORES BETWEEN =68-75
TOP 5: 207-217; Top 10: 218-221

# #3 LEVEL (20-29 STARS)

*EASIEST ONES TO GET INTO, IN DESCENDING ORDER*
## EaglesDream Golf Academy Junior Championship

Boys initial tournament field required a status of **_20_** Performance Stars or more to gain entry; **_3_** Boys with **_19_** Performance Stars gained entry via PBE tiebreaker.
TOP 5: 144-147; Top 10: 149-151

## Amino Vital® / Joey D Golf Junior Championship

Boys initial tournament field required a status of **_21_** Performance Stars or more to gain entry; **_1_** Boy with **_20_** Performance Stars gained entry via PBE tiebreaker.

TOP 5: 141-148; Top 10: 149-151

## ClubCorp Mission Hills Desert Junior

Boys initial tournament field required a status of **_21_** Performance Stars or more to gain entry.

TOP 5: 138-142; Top 10: 144-145

## Justin Thomas Junior Championship

Boys initial tournament field required a status of **_22_** Performance Stars or more to gain entry; **_3_** Boys with **_20_** Performance Stars, the next highest status level, gained entry via PBE tiebreaker.

TOP 5: 217-222; Top 10: 223-226

## Davis Love III Junior Open

Boys initial tournament field required a status of **_23_** Performance Stars or more to gain entry.

QUALIFIER 8 SCORES BETWEEN =67-72

TOP 5: 200-210; Top 10: 211-212

## AJGA Junior at Yolo Fliers

Boys initial tournament field required a status of **_24_** Performance Stars or more to gain entry.

TOP 5: 137-140; Top 10: 142-143

## Jim Bell Memorial Junior presented by PerryGolf

Boys initial tournament field required a status of **_26_** Performance Stars or more to gain entry.
TOP 5: 139-144; Top 10: 145-147

## Sergio Garcia Foundation Junior Championship

Boys initial tournament field required a status of **_29_** Performance Stars or more to gain entry; **_1_** Boy with **_27_** Performance Stars, the next highest status level, gained entry via PBE tiebreaker.
TOP 5: 139-141; Top 10: 142-144

## Puerto Rico Junior Open presented by EaglesDream Golf Academy

Boys initial tournament field required a status of **_29_** Performance Stars or more to gain entry.
TOP 5: 204-207; Top 10: 209-213

# #4 LEVEL (30-39 STARS)

*EASIEST ONES TO GET INTO, IN DESCENDING ORDER*

## Under Armour® / Hunter Mahan Championship presented by Baylor Medical Center at Frisco

Boys initial tournament field required a status of **_30_** Performance Stars or more to gain entry.
TOP 5: 142-145; Top 10: 146-147

## Bishops Gate Golf Academy Junior at Horseshoe Bay

Boys initial tournament field required a status of **_31_** Performance Stars or more to gain entry.

QUALIFIER 8 SCORES BETWEEN 72-78
TOP 5: (212-220); Top 10: (221-223)

## PDQ / Philadelphia Runner Junior
Boys initial tournament field required a status of **_32_** Performance Stars or more to gain entry.
TOP 5: 213-216; Top 10: 217-218

## Callaway Golf Junior Championship
Boys initial tournament field required a status of **_32_** Performance Stars or more to gain entry.
QUALIFIER 11 SCORES BETWEEN =68-75
TOP 5: 208-213; Top 10: 216-217

# #6 LEVEL (50-59 STARS)

*EASIEST ONES TO GET INTO, IN DESCENDING ORDER*
## Wells Fargo Junior Classic presented by Callaway Golf
Boys initial tournament field required a status of **_51_** Performance Stars or more to gain entry.
*TOP 5: 170-178; Top 10: 179-180 **{45 HOLES}**

## Winn Grips Heather Farr Classic hosted by Longbow Golf Club
Boys initial tournament field required a status of **_55_** Performance Stars or more to gain entry; **_1_** Boy with **_51_** Performance Stars, the next highest status level, gained entry via PBE tiebreaker.
QUALIFIER 8 SCORES BETWEEN 70-73
TOP 5: 208-209; Top 10: 210-211

# #7 LEVEL (60-69 STARS)

*EASIEST ONES TO GET INTO, IN DESCENDING ORDER*
**Under Armour® / Jordan Spieth Championship presented by American Campus Communities**
Boys initial tournament field required a status of **64** Performance Stars or more to gain entry; **1** Boy with **56** Performance Stars, the next highest status level, gained entry via PBE tiebreaker.
QUALIFIER 12 SCORES BETWEEN =62-76
TOP 5: 214-218; Top 10: 219-220

# FULLY EXEMPT

**TaylorMade-adidas Golf Junior at Innisbrook hosted by Justin Rose**
Boys initial tournament field - 79 Boys — **FULLY EXEMPT** status gained entry via PBE tiebreaker.
QUALIFIER 9 SCORES BETWEEN 70-73
TOP 5: (216-221); Top 10: (222-223)

# BOYS SENIOR EVENT

**AJGA Senior Showcase Innisbrook Resort & Golf Club**
Boys initial tournament field required a status of **4** Performance Stars or more to gain entry; **9** Boys with **3** Performance Stars gained entry via tiebreaker.
TOP 5: 214-219; Top 10: 221-225

# GIRLS PREVIEW (1 PER NEW MEMBER)

*LISTED IN ORDER OF EASIEST TO HARDEST*

**AJGA Preview at Carolina Trace**
Girls initial tournament field: ***All members*** with 0 tournament opportunities gained entry.
TOP 3:153-155

**AJGA Preview at Cypress Ridge**
Girls initial tournament field: ***All members*** with 0 tournament opportunities gained entry.
TOP 3: 145-147

**AJGA Preview at River Ridge**
Girls initial tournament field: ***All 2016, 2017, 2018, 2019, and 2020*** graduates with 0 tournament opportunities gained entry. ***Four 2021*** graduates with 0 tournament opportunities gained entry via tiebreaker.
TOP 3: 145-151

**AJGA Preview at Ocala**
Girls initial tournament field: ***All 2016, 2017, 2018, and 2019*** graduates with 0 tournament opportunities gained entry. ***Five 2020*** graduates with 0 tournament opportunities gained entry via tiebreaker.
TOP 3: 152-154

## AJGA Preview at Cimarron Hills
Girls initial tournament field: ***All 2016, 2017, 2018, and 2019*** graduates with 0 tournament opportunities gained entry. ***Three 2020*** graduates with 0 tournament opportunities gained entry via tiebreaker.
<u>TOP 3</u>: 154-162

## AJGA Preview at Château Élan presented by Halski Systems
Girls initial tournament field: ***All 2017 & 2018*** graduates with 0 tournament opportunities gained entry. ***Five 2019*** graduates with 0 tournament opportunities gained entry via tiebreaker.
<u>TOP 3</u>: 147-153

## AJGA Preview at Dauphin Highlands
Girls initial tournament field: ***All 2016, 2017, and 2018*** graduates with 0 tournament opportunities gained entry. ***One 2019*** graduate with 0 tournament opportunities gained entry via tiebreaker.
<u>TOP 3</u>: 148-158

## AJGA Preview at Worthington Manor
Girls initial tournament field: ***All 2017 & 2018*** graduates with 0 tournament opportunities gained entry. ***One 2019*** graduate with 0 tournament opportunities gained entry via tiebreaker.
<u>TOP 3</u>: 156-162

## AJGA Preview at The Glen Club
Girls initial tournament field: ***All 2016 & 2017*** graduates with 0 tournament opportunities gained entry. ***Twelve 2018***

graduates with 0 tournament opportunities gained entry via tiebreaker.

TOP 3: 157-162

## AJGA Preview at Brookhaven

Girls initial tournament field: ***All 2016 & 2017*** graduates with 0 tournament opportunities gained entry. ***Four 2018*** graduates with 0 tournament opportunities gained entry via tiebreaker.

TOP 3: 158-164

## AJGA Preview at Sugar Valley

Girls initial tournament field: ***All 2017*** graduates with 0 tournament opportunities gained entry. ***Nine 2018*** graduates with 0 tournament opportunities gained entry via tiebreaker.

TOP 3: 158-160

## AJGA Preview at Innisbruck

Girls initial tournament field: ***All 2017*** graduates with 0 tournament opportunities gained entry. ***Three 2018*** graduates with 0 tournament opportunities gained entry via tiebreaker.

TOP 3: 148-156

## AJGA Preview at Innisbrook (Ages 12-15)

Girls initial tournament field: ***All 2018 and 2019*** graduates with 0 tournament opportunities gained entry. ***One 2020*** graduate with 0 tournament opportunities gained entry via tiebreaker.

TOP 3: 150-153

## AJGA Preview at Morongo (Ages 12-15)

Girls initial tournament field: ***All 2018 and 2019*** graduates with 0 tournament opportunities gained entry.

TOP 3: 150-153

## GIRLS JUNIOR ALL-STAR (AGES 12-15)

## AJGA Junior All-Star at Mooring

Girls initial tournament field : All Girls who applied gained entry

TOP 3: 210-217

AJGA Junior All-Star at Lost Springs presented by Visit Bentonville

Girls initial tournament field required a status of **2** Performance Stars or more to gain entry; **4** Girls with **1** Performance Star gained entry via PBE tiebreaker.

TOP 3: 203-221

## Cameron McCormick Junior All-Star

Girls initial tournament field required a status of **2** Performance Stars or more to gain entry; **2** Girls with **1** Performance Star gained entry via PBE tiebreaker.

TOP 3: 216-217

## Windham Mountain Resort Junior All-Star

Girls initial tournament field required a status of **2** Performance Stars or more to gain entry; **2** Girls with 1 Performance Star gained entry via PBE tiebreaker.

QUALIFIER: 1 QUALIFYING SCORE OF =78
TOP 3: 225-229

## AJGA Junior All-Star at Diablo Grande

Girls initial tournament field required a status of **3** Performance Stars or more to gain entry; **4** Girls with **2** Performance Stars gained entry via PBE tiebreaker.
QUALIFIER: 3 SCORES OF 74-82-90
TOP 3: 210-212

## AJGA Junior All-Star at Rush Creek

Girls initial tournament field required a status of **4** Performance Stars or more to gain entry; **4** Girls with **3** Performance Stars gained entry via PBE tiebreaker.
QUALIFIER: 1=79
TOP 3: 220-224

## AJGA Junior All-Star at Spring Valley

Girls initial tournament field required a status of **4** Performance Stars or more to gain entry; **3** Girls with **3** Performance Stars gained entry via PBE tiebreaker.
QUALIFIER: 1=74
TOP 3: 219-225

## Evitt Foundation RTC Junior All-Star

Girls initial tournament field required a status of **5** Performance Stars or more to gain entry.
QUALIFIER: 2 SCORES OF 75, 78
TOP 3: 223-225

## AJGA Junior All-Star at Bentwater
Girls initial tournament field required a status of **4** Performance Stars or more to gain entry.
TOP 3: 143-146

## Core Golf Academy Junior All-Star
Girls initial tournament field required a status of **6** Performance Stars or more to gain entry; **2** Girls with **5** Performance Stars gained entry via PBE tiebreaker.
QUALIFIER: 1=76
TOP 3: 223-225

## Mill Creek Foundation Junior All-Star
Girls initial tournament field required a status of **6** Performance Stars or more to gain entry; **1** Girl with **5** Performance Stars gained entry via PBE tiebreaker.
QUALIFIER: 3 SCORES OF 71,73, 73
TOP 3: 204-211

## AJGA Junior All-Star at The Virtues
Girls initial tournament field required a status of **6** Performance Stars or more to gain entry; **1** Girl with **5** Performance Stars gained entry via PBE tiebreaker.
TOP 3: 223-225

## AJGA Junior All-Star at Forsgate presented by the Spinnaker Foundation

Girls initial tournament field required a status of **7** Performance Stars or more to gain entry; **1** Girl with **6** Performance Stars gained entry via PBE tiebreaker.

TOP 3: 143-146

## AJGA Junior All-Star at El Conquistador

Girls initial tournament field required a status of **7** Performance Stars or more to gain entry; **2** Girls with **6** Performance Stars gained entry via PBE tiebreaker.

TOP 3: 218-226

AJGA Junior All-Star at Chantilly National

Girls initial tournament field required a status of **8** Performance Stars or more to gain entry; **1** Girl with **5** Performance Stars, the next highest status level, gained entry via PBE tiebreaker.

QUALIFIER: 2 SCORES OF 74,75)

TOP 3: 214-217

# GIRLS OPEN TOURNAMENT (AGES 12-18)

*<Insert #1 LEVEL (1-9 STARS)>*

## Coca-Cola Junior Championship at Sugarloaf

Girls initial tournament field required a status of **3** Performance Stars or more to gain entry; **4** Girls with **2** Performance Stars gained entry via PBE tiebreaker.

TOP 3: 222-232; Top 5: 233

## Sunriver Junior Open
Girls initial tournament field required a status of **_3_** Performance Stars or more to gain entry.
TOP 3: 217-218; Top 5: 219-220

## AJGA Kansas Junior at Buffalo Dunes
Girls initial tournament field required a status of **_4_** Performance Stars or more to gain entry; **_2_** Girls with **_3_** Performance Stars gained entry via PBE tiebreaker.
TOP 3: 211-225; Top 5: 226-227
AJGA Junior at Centennial
Girls initial tournament field required a status of **_4_** Performance Stars or more to gain entry; **_1_** Girl with **_3_** Performance Stars gained entry via PBE tiebreaker.
QUALIFIER: 1=70
TOP 3: 211-212; Top 5: 214-215

## AJGA Junior at Oak Tree
Girls initial tournament field required a status of **_4_** Performance Stars or more to gain entry.
QUALIFIER: 2 SCORES OF 79,81
TOP 3: 208-215; Top 5: 217

## Action Zone / Bob Estes Abilene Junior
Girls initial tournament field required a status of **_4_** Performance Stars or more to gain entry.
QUALIFIER: 1=75
TOP 3: 214-223; Top 5: 224-225

## Natural Resource Partners Bluegrass Junior hosted by J.B. Holmes

Girls initial tournament field required a status of **5** Performance Stars or more to gain entry; **3** Girls with **4** Performance Stars gained entry via PBE tiebreaker.
QUALIFIER: 2 SCORES OF 70,77
TOP 3: 217-223; Top 5: 226

## Killington Junior Golf Championship

Girls initial tournament field required a status of **5** Performance Stars or more to gain entry; **2** Girls with **4** Performance Stars gained entry via PBE tiebreaker.
QUALIFIER: 2 SCORES OF 72,75
TOP 3: 213-214; Top 5: 219

## AJGA City of London Junior Championship

Girls initial tournament field required a status of **5** Performance Stars or more to gain entry; **1** Girl with **4** Performance Stars gained entry via PBE tiebreaker.
QUALIFIER: 2 SCORES 75,76
TOP 3: 209-217; Top 5: 220-222

## Coca-Cola Junior Championship at Boyne Highlands

Girls initial tournament field required a status of **5** Performance Stars or more to gain entry.
QUALIFIER: 2 SCOES OF 73,75
TOP 3: 216-219; Top 5: 220-222

## Wincraft / McArthur Towel & Sports Future Legends
Girls initial tournament field required a status of **5** Performance Stars or more to gain entry.
QUALIFIER: 1=80
TOP 3: 227-231; Top 5: 234-237

## E-Z-GO Vaughn Taylor Championship presented by PotashCorp
Girls initial tournament field required a status of **5** Performance Stars or more to gain entry.
QUALIFIER: 1=76
TOP 3: 211-228; Top 5: 230

## AJGA Junior at The Legends
Girls initial tournament field required a status of **6** Performance Stars or more to gain entry; **1** Girl with **4** Performance Stars, the next highest status level, gained entry via PBE tiebreaker.
QUALIFIER: 2 SCORES 83,85
TOP 3: 220-226; Top 5: 231-233

## AJGA Shanshan Feng Junior Championship
Girls initial tournament field required a status of **6** Performance Stars or more to gain entry.
QUALIFIER: 3 SCORES OF 71,75,78
TOP 3: 214-223; Top 5: 224

## AJGA Huntsville Junior
Girls initial tournament field required a status of **6** Performance Stars or more to gain entry.

QUALIFIER: 2 SCORES OF 79,84
TOP 3: 206-216; Top 5: 217

## Under Armour® Canadian Championship

Girls initial tournament field required a status of **_7_** Performance Stars or more to gain entry; **_2_** Girls with **_5_** Performance Stars, the next highest status level, gained entry via PBE tiebreaker.
QUALIFIER: 1=90
TOP 3: 217-220; Top 5: 221-222

## David Toms Foundation Shreveport Junior

Girls initial tournament field required a status of **_7_** Performance Stars or more to gain entry; **_2_** Girls with **_5_** Performance Stars, the next highest status level, gained entry via PBE tiebreaker.
QUALIFIER: 1=74
TOP 3: 209-222; Top 5: NO TOP-5; THREE T3

## Valero Junior Texas Open

Girls initial tournament field required a status of **_7_** Performance Stars or more to gain entry; **_1_** Girl with **_6_** Performance Stars gained entry via PBE tiebreaker.
QUALIFIER: 2 SCORES OF 76-77
TOP 3: 232-236; Top 5: 237-238

## Bass Pro Shops / Payne Stewart Junior Championship

Girls initial tournament field required a status of **_7_** Performance Stars or more to gain entry.
TOP 3: 214-216; Top 5: 221-226

## EaglesDream Golf Academy Junior Open
Girls initial tournament field required a status of **7** Performance Stars or more to gain entry.
QUALIFIER: 3 SCORES OF 72,77,77
TOP 3: 216-221; Top 5: 223

## Greg Norman Champions Golf Academy Junior Championship
Girls initial tournament field required a status of **8** Performance Stars or more to gain entry; **1** Girl with **7** Performance Stars gained entry via PBE tiebreaker.
QUALIFIER: 3 SCORES OF 75,77,77
TOP 3: 216-220; Top 5: 221-227

## AJGA Reno / Tahoe Junior at ArrowCreek
Girls initial tournament field required a status of **8** Performance Stars or more to gain entry; **1** Girl with **7** Performance Stars gained entry via PBE tiebreaker.
QUALIFIER: 2 SCORES OF 75,77
TOP 3: 216-227; Top 5: 228-231

## AJGA Junior at Forest Lake presented by Tom Holzer Ford
Girls initial tournament field required a status of **8** Performance Stars or more to gain entry.
QUALIFIER: 4 SCORES OF 79-88
TOP 3: 228-231; Top 5: NO TOP-5; THREE T3

## New Era Junior Championship

Girls initial tournament field required a status of **8** Performance Stars

QUALIFIER: 2 SCORES OF 81

TOP 3: 213-218; Top 5: 223

## Judie Oppenheimer Memorial Junior

Girls initial tournament field required a status of **9** Performance Stars or more to gain entry; **3** Girls with **7** Performance Stars, the next highest status level, gained entry via PBE tiebreaker.

QUALIFIER: 1=77

TOP 3: 219-220; Top 5: 228-229

## Under Armour® / Scott Stallings Championship presented by Pilot Flying J

Girls initial tournament field required a status of **9** Performance Stars or more to gain entry.

QUALIFIER: 4 SCORES BETWEEN OF 79-82

TOP 3: 213-217; Top 5: 220

## IZOD AJGA Championship

Girls initial tournament field required a status of **9** Performance Stars or more to gain entry.

QUALIFIER: 1=75

TOP 3: 209-216; Top 5: 217-218

# <INSERT #2 LEVEL (10-19 STARS)>

## *EASIEST ONES TO GET INTO, IN DESCENDING ORDER*
### Ryan Moore Junior Championship at Anthem
Girls initial tournament field required a status of **_10_** Performance Stars or more to gain entry; **_1_** Girl with **_7_** Performance Stars, the next highest status level, gained entry via PBE tiebreaker.
<u>QUALIFIER</u>: 3 SCORES OF BETWEEN 73-75
<u>TOP 3</u>: 213-219; <u>Top 5</u>: 221

### AJGA Junior at Owensboro
Girls initial tournament field required a status of **_10_** Performance Stars or more to gain entry; **_1_** Girl with **_9_** Performance Stars gained entry via PBE tiebreaker.
<u>QUALIFIER</u>: 3 SCORES OF 78,82,83
<u>TOP 3</u>: (217-225); <u>Top 5</u>: 226-227

### St. Francisville Area Foundation Junior at The Bluffs
Girls initial tournament field required a status of **_10_** Performance Stars or more to gain entry.
<u>QUALIFIER</u>: 3 SCORES OF 78,82,83
<u>TOP 3</u>: (209-216); <u>Top 5</u>: (217-218)

### Junior Golf Hub Championship
Girls initial tournament field required a status of **_10_** Performance Stars or more to gain entry.
<u>QUALIFIER</u>: 3 SCORES OF 70-75-76
<u>TOP 3</u>: 210-219; <u>Top 5</u>: 220

Insperity Invitational / Patrick Reed AJGA Junior Championship
**presented by Callaway Golf**
Girls initial tournament field required a status of **_11_** Performance Stars or more to gain entry.
QUALIFIER: 3 SCORES OF 73-75-77
TOP 3: 218-224; Top 5: 226-227

**the Memorial Junior presented by Ohio Christian University**
Girls initial tournament field required a status of **_11_** Performance Stars or more to gain entry.
QUALIFIER: 3 SCORES OF 71-76-76
TOP 3: 217-222; Top 5: 224

**Lockton Kansas City Junior**
Girls initial tournament field required a status of **_11_** Performance Stars or more to gain entry.
QUALIFIER: 2 SCORES OF 75,78
TOP 3: 221-224; Top 5: 226

**ACDS / Ryan Moore Junior at Oakbrook**
Girls initial tournament field required a status of **_12_** Performance Stars or more to gain entry; **_1_** Girl with **_11_** Performance Stars gained entry via PBE tiebreaker.
QUALIFIER: 3 SCORES OF 77,78,80
TOP 3: 212-215; Top 5: 216

## FORE Performance Junior Championship
Girls initial tournament field required a status of **_12_** Performance Stars or more to gain entry.
QUALIFIER: 2 SCORES OF 74-75
TOP 3: 208-216; Top 5: 219-222

Randy Wise Junior Open
Girls initial tournament field required a status of **_12_** Performance Stars or more to gain entry.
QUALIFIER: 2 SCORES OF 72,76
TOP 3: 213-225; Top 5: 227-228

## Lessing's AJGA Classic
Girls initial tournament field required a status of **_13_** Performance Stars or more to gain entry.
QUALIFIER: 2 SCORES OF 71,74
TOP 3: 214-222; Top 5: 226

## PING Phoenix Junior at ASU Kirsten
Girls initial tournament field required a status of **_14_** Performance Stars or more to gain entry.
QUALIFIER: 2 SCORES OF 75-76
TOP 3: 207-216; Top 5: 217-219

AJGA Junior at The Ranch
Girls initial tournament field required a status of **_15_** Performance Stars or more to gain entry.
QUALIFIER: 2 SCORES OF 75
TOP 3: 213-218; Top 5: 219-221

## Under Armour® / Gary Woodland Championship

Girls initial tournament field required a status of **_15_** Performance Stars or more to gain entry.

QUALIFIER: 2 SCORES OF 73-75
TOP 3: 220-223; Top 5: 227-230

## AJGA Junior at Carlton Oaks

Girls initial tournament field required a status of **_16_** Performance Stars or more to gain entry.

TOP 3: 139-143; Top 5: 145

## Daniel Berger Junior Championship

Girls initial tournament field required a status of **_16_** Performance Stars or more to gain entry.

QUALIFIER: 2 SCORES OF 75-77
TOP 3: 222-224; Top 5: 226-227

## PDQ / Philadelphia Runner Junior

Girls initial tournament field required a status of **_17_** Performance Stars or more to gain entry; **_1_** Girl with **_15_** Performance Stars, the next highest status level, gained entry via PBE tiebreaker.

QUALIFIER: 2 SCORES OF 74,76
TOP 3: 211-217; Top 5: 222-224

## AJGA Junior at Cattail Creek

Girls initial tournament field required a status of **_17_** Performance Stars or more to gain entry; **_1_** Girl with **_16_** Performance Stars gained entry via PBE tiebreaker.

QUALIFIER: 2 SCORES OF 69,76
TOP 3: 212-220; Top 5: 226

## Wells Fargo Junior Classic presented by Hallway Golf
Girls initial tournament field required a status of **_18_** Performance Stars or more to gain entry.
TOP 3: 179-183; Top 5: 184

AJGA Hale Irwin Colorado Junior presented by Huntington Industrial Partners
Girls initial tournament field required a status of **_18_** Performance Stars or more to gain entry.
QUALIFIER: 1=72
TOP 3: 209-214; Top 5: 216-217

## Enagic Junior Championship
Girls initial tournament field required a status of **_19_** Performance Stars or more to gain entry.
QUALIFIER: 8 SCORES BETWEEN 71-76
TOP 3: 205-211; Top 5: 214

## AJGA Philadelphia Junior
Girls initial tournament field required a status of **_19_** Performance Stars or more to gain entry.
QUALIFIER: 4 SCORES BETWEEN 74-76
TOP 3: 209-222; Top 5: 225

<Insert #3 LEVEL (20-29 STARS)>

_EASIEST GIRLS' ONES TO GET INTO, IN DESCENDING ORDER_
## Amino Vital® / Joey D Golf Junior Championship

Girls initial tournament field required a status of **_20_** Performance Stars or more to gain entry; **_1_** Girl with **_19_** Performance Stars gained entry via PBE tiebreaker.
TOP 3: 143-144; Top 5: 148-150

## ClubCorp Mission Hills Desert Junior
Girls initial tournament field required a status of **_20_** Performance Stars or more to gain entry.
TOP 3: 142-144; Top 5: 145

## AJGA Junior at Yolo Fliers
Girls initial tournament field required a status of **_21_** Performance Stars or more to gain entry.
TOP 3: 147-148; Top 5: 149

## Callaway Golf Junior Championship
Girls initial tournament field required a status of **_22_** Performance Stars or more to gain entry.
QUALIFIER 3 SCORES OF 73-73-74
TOP 3: 213-215; Top 5: 219

## EaglesDream Golf Academy Junior Championship
Girls initial tournament field required a status of **_23_** Performance Stars or more to gain entry.
TOP 3: 146-149; Top 5: 150

## Rome Junior Classic presented by State Mutual Insurance Company
Girls initial tournament field required a status of **_23_** Performance Stars or more to gain entry.
TOP 3: 139-142; Top 5: 144

## Justin Thomas Junior Championship
Girls initial tournament field required a status of **_23_** Performance Stars or more to gain entry.
<u>TOP 3</u>: 218-224; <u>Top 5</u>: 226

## Davis Love III Junior Open
Girls initial tournament field required a status of **_23_** Performance Stars or more to gain entry.
<u>QUALIFIER 2 SCORES OF 74</u>
<u>TOP 3</u>: 209-215; <u>Top 5</u>: 216-219

## Jim Bell Memorial Junior presented by PerryGolf
Girls initial tournament field required a status of **_25_** Performance Stars or more to gain entry.
<u>TOP 3</u>: 145-147; <u>Top 5</u>: 148-149

*<Insert #4 LEVEL (30-39 STARS)>*

<u>*EASIEST ONES TO GET INTO, IN DESCENDING ORDER*</u>
## AJGA / CJGT Junior at Yorba Linda
Girls initial tournament field required a status of **_33_** Performance Stars or more to gain entry.
<u>QUALIFIER 4 SCORES BETWEEN 72-75</u>
<u>TOP 3</u>: 209-214; <u>Top 5</u>: 215-216

## Bishops Gate Golf Academy Junior at Horseshoe Bay
Girls initial tournament field required a status of **_34_** Performance Stars or more to gain entry.
<u>QUALIFIER 3 SCORES OF 77-81</u>
<u>TOP 3</u>: 212-220; <u>Top 5</u>: 225

Under Armour® / Hunter Mahan Championship presented by
**Baylor Medical Center at Frisco**
Girls initial tournament field required a status of **_35_** Performance
Stars or more to gain entry.
TOP 3: 139-144; Top 5: 148

*<Insert #5 LEVEL (40-49 STARS)>*

*EASIEST ONES TO GET INTO, IN DESCENDING ORDER*
**Winn Grips Heather Farr Classic hosted by Longbow Golf
Club**
Girls initial tournament field required a status of **_40_** Performance
Stars or more to gain entry.
QUALIFIER 2 SCORES OF 73,77
TOP 3: 215-218; Top 5: 219-220

Under Armour® / Jordan Spieth Championship presented by
**American Campus Communities**
Girls initial tournament field required a status of **_46_** Performance
Stars or more to gain entry.
QUALIFIER 4 SCORES BETWEEN 75-79
TOP 3: 215-221; Top 5: 224-227

**Sergio Garcia Foundation Junior Championship**
Girls initial tournament field required a status of **_48_** Performance
Stars or more to gain entry.
TOP 3: 141; Top 5: 145

*<Insert #7 LEVEL (60-69 STARS)>*

## AJGA Girls Championship

Girls initial tournament field required a status of **65** Performance Stars or more to gain entry.

TOP 3: 210-211; Top 5: 212-213

*<Insert FULLY EXEMPT>*

## EASIEST ONES TO GET INTO, IN DESCENDING ORDER

## TaylorMade-adidas Golf Junior at Innisbrook hosted by Justin Rose

Girls initial tournament field - 37 - required **FULLY EXEMPT** status to gain entry; 1 Girl with 54 Performance Stars, the next highest status level, gained entry via PBE tiebreaker.

QUALIFIER 3 SCORES BETWEEN 71-74

TOP 3: 217-220; Top 5: 221

## Under Armour® / Alison Lee Championship

Girls initial tournament field —23 - required **FULLY EXEMPT** status to gain entry.

QUALIFIER 2 SCORES OF 71,78

TOP 3: 216-221

## GIRLS SENIOR EVENT

### AJGA Senior Showcase Innisbrook Resort & Golf Club

All Girls who applied gained entry.

TOP 3: (227-246); TOP 5: (255); *(ONLY **6** ENTERED, SO **3** EARNED **EXEMPT** STATUS; **2** EARNED **12** PERFORMANCE STARS; **1** EARNED **8** PERFORMANCE STARS)*

# References

Ames, Daniel R.; Kammrath, Lara K. (September 2004). "Mind-Reading and Metacognition: Narcissism, not Actual Competence, Predicts Self-Estimated Ability" (PDF). Journal of Nonverbal Behavior 28 (3): 187–209. doi:10.1023/B:JONB.0000039649.20015.

Anders, Ericsson. https://psy.fsu.edu/faculty/ericsson.dp.html.

Axelrod, Dr. Julius. http://www.jbc.org/content/233/3/702.full.pdf+html.

Binmore, Ken. *Does Game Theory Work? The Bargaining Challenge*. Cambridge, MA: MIT Press, 2007.

Bjork, E. L., & Bjork, R. A. (in press). Making things hard on yourself, but in a good way: Creating desirable difficulties to enhance learning. In M. A. Gernsbacher and J. Pomerantz (Eds.), Psychology and the real world: Essays illustrating fundamental contributions to society (2nd edition). New York: Worth.

Bjork Koriat, A., & Bjork, R. A. (2006). Illusions of competence during study can be remedied by manipulations that enhance learners' sensitivity to retrieval conditions at test. Memory & Cognition, 34, 959-972.

Bjork, R. A. (in press). Forgetting as a friend of learning. In D. S. Lindsay, C. M. Kelley, A. P. Yonelinas, & H. L. Roediger, III (Eds.) Remembering: Attributions, processes, and control in human memory: Papers in honour of Larry L. Jacoby. New York: Psychology Press.

Bjork, R. A., & Yan, V. X. (in press). The increasing importance of learning how to learn. Chapter to appear in M.A. McDaniel & G. Frey (Eds.) Integrating Cognitive Science with Innovative Teaching in STEM.

Callender, A.A. & McDaniel, M.A., The Limited Benefits of Rereading Educational texts, Contemporary Educational Psychology, Vol. 34.1, Jan. 2009

Carrell, Scott and West, James.http://www.npr.org/2014/03/26/294639911/air-force-academy-squadrons-test-peer-effect-assumptions.

Cepeda, H. Pashler, Rohrer. Massed vs spacing practice. Psychological bulletin 132 206 354-380.

Duckworth, Angela Lee. http://www.ted.com/talks/angela_lee_duckworth_the_key_to_success_grit.

Dweck, Carole. Growth mindset. http://www.ted.com/talks/carol_dweck_the_power_of_believing_that_you_can_improve.

Dunning, David; Johnson, Kerri; Ehrlinger, Joyce; Kruger, Justin (2003). "Why people fail to recognize their own incompetence" (PDF). Current Directions in Psychological Science 12 (3): 83–87.

Gates, Arthur I. *Recitation as a Factor in Memorizing,*. New York: Science, 1917. Print.

Gladwell, Malcolm. *David and Goliath: Underdogs, Misfits, and the Art of Battling Giants*. New York: Little, Brown and Company, 2013.

Gladwell, Malcolm. *Outliers: The Story of Success*. New York: Little, Brown and Company, 2008.

RCGA: http://www.rcga.org/_uploads/documents/Player percent20Development/LTPD/Golf_In_Canada_low.pdf)

Jackson, C. Kirabo. http://works.bepress.com/c_kirabo_jackson/15/.

Jensen, Rick. *Easier Said than Done: The Undeniable, Tour-Tested Truths that You Must Know (and Apply) to Finally Play to Your Potential on the Golf Course*. Seattle, WA: Sea Script Company, 2010.

Kahneman, Daniel. *Thinking, Fast and Slow.* New York: Farrar, Straus and Giroux, 2011.

Kornell, N., Castel, A. D., Eich, T. S., & Bjork, R. A. (2010). Spacing as the friend of both memory and induction in younger and older adults. Psychology and Aging, 25, 498-503.

Kornell, N., Bjork, R. A., & Garcia, M. A. (2011). Why tests appear to prevent forgetting: A distribution-based bifurcation model. Journal of Memory and Language, 65, 85-97.

Kruger, Justin; Dunning, David (1999). "Unskilled and Unaware of It: How Difficulties in Recognizing One's Own Incompetence Lead to Inflated Self-Assessments". Journal of Personality and Social Psychology 77 (6): 1121–34. doi:10.1037/0022-3514.77.6.1121. PMID 10626367. CiteSeerX: 10.1.1.64.2655.

Larsen, Butler, Lawson. Repeated testing improves long term retention compared to repeated study – Medical Education 43 (2009) 1174-1181.

Low stakes – high frequency improves test taking – Teaching of Psychology 29 (2002) 210-212.

Marshmallow Test Points to Biological Basis for Delayed Gratification". *Science Daily.* September 1, 2011. Archived from the original on October 4, 2011. Retrieved October 4, 2011.

Mazur, Eric, Peer Instruction, A User's Manual, Prentice Hall, NJ, 1997

Merton, R. K. "The Matthew Effect In Science: The Reward And Communication Systems Of Science Are Considered." *Science*: 56-63. Print.

Mischel, Walter; Ebbesen, Ebbe B.; Raskoff Zeiss, Antonette (1972). "Cognitive and attentional mechanisms in delay of gratification.". Journal of Personality and Social Psychology 21 (2): 204–218. doi:10.1037/h0032198. ISSN 0022-3514. PMID 5010404.

Mischel, Walter; Shoda, Yuichi; Rodriguzez, Monica L. (1989). "Delay of gratification in children.". Science 244: 933–938. doi:10.1126/science.2658056

Solving a problem vs remembering a solution – Journal of Verbal Learning and Verbal Behaviour 17 (1978) 649-667

Spitzer, H. F. "Studies in Retention." Journal of Educational Psychology: 641-56. Print.

Storm, B. C., Bjork, E. L., & Bjork, R. A. (2007). When intended remembering leads to unintended forgetting. Quarterly Journal of Experimental Psychology, 60, 909-915.

Storm, B. C., Bjork, R. A., & Storm, J. C. (2010). Optimizing retrieval as a learning event: When and why expanding retrieval practice enhances long-term retention. Memory & Cognition, 38, 244-253.

Svenson, O. (1981). "Are we all less risky and more skillful than our fellow drivers?". Acta Psychologica 47 (2): 143. doi:10.1016/0001-6918(81)90005-6.

Thaler, Richard H. "Anomalies: The Ultimatum Game." *Journal of Economic Perspectives:* 195-206. Print.

Triplet, Norman. http://psychclassics.yorku.ca/Triplett/

Tulving, Endel. "Study of Memory: Processes and Systems." *Memory: Systems, Process, or Function?* (1999): 11-30. Print.

"Why Losers Have Delusions of Grandeur". New York Post. 23 May 2010. Retrieved 19 March 2014.

Wolf, J. H.; Wolf, K. S. (2013). The Lake Wobegon effect: Are all cancer patients above average? Milbank Quarterly 91 (4): 690–728. doi:10.1111/1468-0009.12030. PMC 3876187. PMID 24320166.

Made in the USA
Lexington, KY
21 May 2018